EMPLOYEE ENGAGEMENT

Creating positive energy at work

Joan Peters

TALENT MANAGEMENT SERIES

First published in 2019.

ISBN: 978-1-86922-814-9
eISBN: 978-1-86922-815-6 (ePDF)

Published by KR Publishing
P O Box 3954
Randburg
2125
Republic of South Africa

Tel: (011) 706-6009
Fax: (011) 706-1127
E-mail: orders@knowres.co.za
Website: www.kr.co.za

Typesetting, layout and design: Cia Joubert, cia@knowres.co.za
Cover design: Marlene de'Lorme, marlene@knowres.co.za
Editing and proofreading: Jennifer Renton, jenniferrenton@live.co.za
Project management: Cia Joubert, cia@knowres.co.za

Table of Contents

About the Author

Previously Leadership Development Manager at Volkswagen Group South Africa, today **Joan Peters** is a consultant in the field of leadership and organisational development, as well as an executive coach. She works closely with CEOs and a wide range of executive management, leading a range of change management processes. These include leadership development interventions, coaching, talent management, assessment centres, organisational culture and values interventions, employee engagement surveys and team development workshops. Joan has an M Phil in Management Coaching from the University of Stellenbosch Business School.

Introduction

Highly engaged employees are essential for the success of their organisations. A highly engaged employee will ensure a great customer experience, high quality work, innovations and improved productivity.

As leaders or HR executives, we need a good understanding of the drivers of engagement so we can create the conditions for people to make their greatest contributions at work and be successful as an organisation.

Employee Engagement is a complete how-to book that will help you to implement a sound employee engagement strategy for today's workplace. This book unpacks the role that leaders and HR play in employee engagement, and discusses:

- the importance of employee engagement for organisational success;

- the conditions required for highly engaged employees;

- creating the organisational climate required for high engagement;

- matching work to employee's strengths;

- creating a sense of meaning and purpose at work through an inspiring vision, values and culture;

- supporting employees in their personal and work-related growth and development;

- ensuring leaders play their role in creating high engagement;

- measuring employee engagement; and

- addressing organisational issues for high engagement.

Employee Engagement is essential reading for anyone who manages or leads people currently, or will lead them in the future, as it provides the necessary tools to ensure people will want to do their best work. *Employee Engagement* is also intended for HR executives who are responsible for crafting employee policies. Finally, individual employees will gain great insights from this book into the factors affecting their own engagement at work.

Who is this book for?

This book is intended for the HR Business Partner, Learning and Development Practitioner and the Line Manager who want to create the conditions for high employee engagement. The objective is to offer broad guidelines on implementing employee engagement initiatives. This book is aimed at providing a thorough understanding of the leadership principles that support employee engagement, as well as ways in which HR can support the leadership of their organisations in creating an environment where employees can do their best work. I have also included references for some literature and a few websites that provide more depth into some of the concepts I cover.

I have made use of the two genders interchangeably in the book to prevent any perception of gender bias. In addition, I have included checklists and reflective exercises to help you think through how you could apply these principles at your workplace.

Using this book

This book follows the Employee Engagement Practice Flow Chart on page viii. There are three main sections to the book: Section 1 covers the reasons for the focus on employee engagement; Section 2 examines the leader's role in creating a workplace culture and climate for high engagement; and Section 3 focuses on HR's supporting role in employee engagement initiatives.

A Model for Employee Engagement

Section 1

Why focus on employee engagement?

Chapter 1

High levels of employee engagement benefit everyone

In this chapter we will explore the following topics:

- The challenges we face as HR and as leaders in companies.
- The reasons why employee engagement has become a high priority for organisations.
- How companies prioritise the importance of the customer, the shareholder and the employee.
- The changing expectations that employees have of their employers.
- What we mean by the term "employee engagement".
- Is employee engagement the same as employee satisfaction?
- The term "Employee Experience" is used often. Is that the same as employee engagement?
- Is "engagement" just another term for "workaholism"?
- Can the impact of employee engagement on company performance be quantified?
- How important is it to employees that they feel highly engaged at work?
- How does work contribute to well-being?
- How well are companies doing when it comes to employee engagement?
- Reflective questions.

The challenges we face

Rochelle leaned back in her chair as her team left her office after their weekly meeting. She was feeling uneasy. Rochelle was new to her company, RoofCo, a manufacturer of roof tiles, having only joined two months ago. She headed up the Marketing team, which was responsible for functions such as sales forecasts, identifying sales outlets, market research, promotions and advertising.

Rochelle had inherited a small team of talented and well-qualified people. Two team members were over the age of 45 and had great knowledge and experience with the company. This should have made them an excellent support to the four younger employees who were below the age of 35. Rochelle's expectations were that team meetings and one-on-one meetings should generate lively discussions and many ideas, and that people should be energised in their roles and willing to take on projects and test ideas.

So far this was not the case, however. Meetings were fairly quiet; only one or two employees offered any ideas and people seemed to be waiting for instructions. There was a strange, cautious atmosphere with little initiative and low energy. Rochelle was wondering what her strategy should be to build higher levels of energy amongst her team. The goals for the department were tough, so she needed everyone to be fully engaged and to collaborate, innovate and achieve the targets she had agreed to.

Meanwhile, 20 kms away in the industrial area, the CEO of Rozzby, Daniel, was preparing for a Board meeting. His frustration level was rising as he worked through the numbers; customer satisfaction was down, absences were edging higher and warranty costs were rising, which was no surprise as the in-house quality management system was highlighting many faults picked up at the end of the production line, despite the extra quality checking stations they had installed. There was constant conflict between the people in the production, quality and engineering divisions. Employee turnover was low, but in the past three months, four of the company's top talent had resigned. It seemed to Daniel that his employees just did not care about the company or the quality of their work.

In a thoroughly bad mood, he phoned Laurisha, the HR Director. "Looking at company performance figures, I would say we have a people problem. And don't tell me we don't pay people enough. We pay above the market rate! We've upgraded the facilities on the line as well as the offices. We introduced flexible work hours for the office staff and the managers received great bonuses. It seems to me people just don't care about the company, the product or the customer. And the people we recruited at great cost to help us turn the situation around are also resigning. There's no loyalty anymore. We have a Board meeting coming up so I am putting you on the agenda to give the HR view on this and recommend a way forward."

Employee engagement has become a high priority for organisations

As a leader in your company or as a Human Resources leader, I am sure you can relate to these scenarios. The challenge for leadership and HR is how to consistently get the best performance from employees so that the company can achieve its targets of productivity, customer experience, product quality and profitability. The business environment is certainly tough for most companies: customers are more demanding, the economy is sluggish, new competitors and technologies can suddenly emerge and disrupt the business, product life cycles are shorter as customers head off to buy the latest novelty, customer service must wow the customer, not just satisfy them, and products need to be manufactured faster, cheaper and better.

The customer, the shareholder and the employee

Traditionally, companies placed a high priority on the importance of the shareholder and the customer to the business. Leadership believed that for the business to be successful and profitable, the organisation needed to focus on their customers' experience of doing business with the company and keeping the shareholders happy.

Then there was the realisation that the company's employees determined the customers' experience. A good customer experience is the result of engaged employees throughout the value chain. Think of every group of employees in a business who have an impact on customer experience, directly or indirectly. These include employees who:

- designed, made and sold the product

- managed the customer's account;

- recruited and trained the employees in the business so they were able to do a good job;

- set up the production lines, ordered parts and got them to the line on time;

- developed business processes and systems;

- managed and motivated others;

- cleaned the offices; and

- paid the staff.

Every employee contributes to the quality of the product or the service experienced by the customer, and the customer's experience is the deciding factor on whether or not he or she will continue to do business with that company.

The Gallup organisation conducted research that supports the view that employee engagement is an important factor in organisational success. Their view is that "engaged workers are the lifeblood of their organizations" and to win customers, companies need to win the hearts and minds of their employees.[1]

Leadership and Team	My job	Great Employee Experience	Engaged Employee	My job
Connection Support Trust	Aligned to my strengths Purpose and meaning Growth and development	Belonging Achievement Well-being	Great job performance Initiative	

Figure 1: Employee Experience and Customer Experience

If engaged employees lead to engaged customers, companies need to focus on how to engage their employees, meaning the employees' experience at work becomes an important topic for business leaders. We need to reflect on how we create an employee experience that leads to engaged employees.

In practice...

Richard Branson was able to build Virgin into a global powerhouse by focusing on customer service, yet he revealed that Virgin does not put the customer first. In fact, Virgin employees are the company's top priority. As Branson sees it, the formula is very simple: Happy employees equal happy customers. Similarly, an unhappy employee can ruin the brand experience for not just one, but numerous customers.

"If the person who works at your company is not appreciated, they are not going to do things with a smile," Branson says. By not treating employees well, companies risk losing customers due to bad service. Branson says he has made sure that Virgin prioritises employees first, customers second, and shareholders third. "Effectively, in the end shareholders do well, the customers do better, and your staff remains happy," he says.[2]

Employee engagement has thus become a high priority for all organisations, as for a company to be successful in a tough business environment, it needs highly competent and highly engaged employees who can meet the employer's high expectations of them.

These include:

- making sure the customer has a memorable experience;

- being innovative and making the product more appealing,

- creating better quality and less expensive to manufacture products;

- being results-driven, hard-working and quick;

- staying up-to-date with rapid changes in the field;

- being collaborative;

- being flexible; and

- keeping their phones on so the company can contact them when they are not at the workplace.

The general belief is that when people are engaged and love their work, they do better work. According to a survey conducted by HR.com, over 90% of respondents believed that there is solid evidence linking engagement to performance, and that engagement has the strongest impact on customer service and productivity.[3]

In addition, according to executives at the World's Most Admired Companies, a list prepared by *Fortune* magazine and Korn Ferry, an engaged workforce is essential to effectively cope with change. "Engaged employees are more willing to accept and embrace the organizational changes needed to address customer concerns and cost issues."[4]

For all these reasons, the issues of retention and employee engagement have become high priority issues for business leaders. As employers' expectations of employees increase, so do employees' expectations of their employers. According to research undertaken by Deloitte, the employee work contract has changed.[5] Talented employees are in a strong position, the job market is highly transparent, and companies are competing for highly skilled employees. However, as employers' expectations of employees increase, so do employees' expectations of their employers.

Talent in the form of well-educated and tech-savvy people is generally not daunted by a demanding work situation. Many of these people have the approach of, "I would love to be part of the business challenge. It sounds exciting. I want to be challenged and to be part of exciting projects. However, I have my own expectations of the Company as my employer and of my leadership. The salary and benefits are important to me but my needs are greater than that. I am looking at the total work experience and things like meaningful work, the opportunity to be creative, ongoing development, inspiring leadership, recognition and a sense of belonging are also important if you want the best out of me".

Talent in the form of the worker on the shop floor who is now working with sophisticated equipment and expected to turn out top quality work that would have been unthinkable a few years ago is also typically saying, "I am proud to be working at this company and I love the product. However, if you want the best out of me, please don't treat me like a number or as an extension of the machine. Talk to me, listen to my ideas and concerns, address my problems with parts and equipment, respect me, get to know me, support me and involve me".

Talent in the form of the older, wiser, more experienced and possibly less-qualified employees also has needs. They are saying, "Change and new demands are all happening rapidly, so I need support and reassurance. I have been doing a good job for years, I like my team, we've been together for a long time, and I don't always agree that there is a need to change. For me, the old way still works fine, but if things need to change, please make sure I get the necessary training and the time I need to adjust".

The challenge for leaders is to provide a work experience that brings out the best in all their people, which means more focus on the intangible factors that affect the way people feel about their work. This is often not familiar territory for many leaders, and is certainly an important aspect in our development and growth as leaders.

What do we mean by the term "employee engagement"?

There is no single definition of employee engagement, but there is wide agreement that it is an emotional commitment to one's work and a willingness to give of one's best at work. It is how people feel about their work that determines their levels of energy, ownership, persistence, commitment and initiative.

Signs of high engagement include:

- the extent to which employees commit to achieving results and how hard they work;
- a passion and purpose for what they do and a sense that they are contributing to something bigger than themselves, i.e. they want to make a positive difference to something;
- how much initiative people take;
- how long they stay in the organisation;
- a high level of innovation and effort to assist a company or unit in the company to reach its goals/strategy;
- the high, positive energy and enthusiasm with which people approach their work;
- the level of ownership and involvement with their work that people display;
- a willingness to take on a new challenge;
- a receptiveness and openness to change;
- the high standards people set for themselves in terms of their conduct at work, the quality of their work and the pride people take in their work;
- a focus on the customer or client and meeting their needs;
- efforts made to learn more about their field so they can do more and be more innovative;

- a willingness to be collaborative with colleagues in an effort to leverage others' skills and the inputs that are needed to deliver a quality result or to solve a problem quickly;

- how long a person perseveres when things are not going well; and

- the extent to which people are prepared to "go the extra mile". When employees care, i.e. when they are engaged, they put in the extra effort needed to resolve a customer's problem, make sure the new process is working, or sort out a quality problem on the line.

This is referred to as "discretionary effort"; it is the level of effort people could give if they wanted to, above and beyond the minimum required. I can recall many examples of discretionary effort by employees, such as maintenance teams who worked through the night to get a vital piece of equipment working or a logistics employee who drove at night to the supplier's warehouse to fetch critically needed parts to keep the production line going. In one case, a supplier had a fire at their premises so employees from the customer company volunteered to work at the supplier over the weekend to help them get their production going again.

Engagement levels influence a person's willingness to go the extra mile at work. Engaged employees put in discretionary effort because they love their job and want to see their company succeed! Disengaged employees drag our business down. You will recognise the disengaged employee as they:

- tend to do the minimum;

- display low energy levels;

- are often negative or cynical, especially about any proposed changes;

- see the customer or client as simply too demanding;

- are not interested in learning and innovation as it looks like too much of an effort;

- want to reduce their role and responsibilities rather than expand them; and

- have a negative impact on the team climate: younger employees tend to wonder if this is how you should be at work? Is this disengaged person maybe showing them the realities of work and how to survive?

It is very sad, of course, if your disengaged team member was once full of positive energy and has been closed down by bad experiences at work.

The bottom line is, your employees can come to work every day, but if they aren't truly engaged in their work, they are harming your business in some way as mediocrity and minimal effort become the norm. Many organisations struggle with employees who are at work, but not fully contributing.

Is employee engagement the same as employee satisfaction?

Engagement is a feeling; it's an emotional commitment to your work and comes about as a reaction to the intangible factors at work. Satisfaction, on the other hand, is based more on an employee's rational assessment of the tangible workplace issues. If we map ENGAGEMENT and SATISFACTION as two separate topics, we can come up with the following scenarios:

SATISFACTION	HIGH	High satisfaction/low engagement	High satisfaction/high engagement
	LOW	Low satisfaction/low engagement	High engagement/low satisfaction
		LOW	HIGH
		ENGAGEMENT	

Figure 2: Satisfaction and engagement scenarios

High satisfaction/low engagement: Have you ever felt like the person who says this?

My job ticks all the boxes:	
▣ I earn a good salary.	✓
▣ I work for a company with a great reputation and product.	✓
▣ I have an impressive job title.	✓
▣ I have a beautiful office.	✓
▣ I have a great laptop and cell phone.	✓
▣ I enjoy high status at work and in my community.	✓

However, I really cannot say that I love my job. In fact, I feel a little depressed at the start of the work week and I have to talk sternly to myself. I am paying off a house and car and my kids' education is expensive. Plus, I have to save for retirement one day, so I need this job with its perks and benefits, and I enjoy the status it gives me in my family and community.

This scenario is sometimes referred to as "golden handcuffs". Looking at this person's work situation from the outside, one may feel a little envious and think this person has it made, yet high satisfaction alone does not lead to high engagement or mean you love your work. Many people start off their career aiming to achieve these factors, only to find that there are other intangible factors pulling at them. They may achieve their goals in terms of money and status, for example, but still feel something is missing. The relationship between the tangibles and the intangibles is actually more complicated than we realise.

Low satisfaction/low engagement: Being dissatisfied and disengaged is the worst scenario for the company and the employee! This person will hate coming to work and will radiate negativity. This is a no-win situation: the customer and colleagues will all have a bad experience dealing with this person.

High engagement/low satisfaction: This is the "flight risk" scenario. In this scenario a person would say: "I love:

- the work that I do;
- the challenges I face and the problems I solve;
- the difference I make;
- the colleagues and the leaders I work with;
- the positive environment I experience at work; and
- the sense of achievement."

This person loves the work but feels the company is taking advantage of them. They feel they are giving a lot and are not appreciated or sufficiently valued in return in terms of salary, seniority or other tangible benefits. This person will soon be looking around for a new position and when they resign, there is often a quick scramble to make a counter-offer in the hopes of retaining their skills and positive energy.

High satisfaction/high engagement: This is the best scenario for the company and the employee. The person loves the work they do and feels fairly compensated and acknowledged by the business.

Many people confuse engagement with satisfaction and try to remedy engagement problems with solutions like pay increases, better offices, gym memberships, fixing the employee car park, improving the canteen, introducing concierge services and so on. These solutions do have an impact on satisfaction, but more satisfaction does not lead to more engagement. It is the equivalent of trying to buy love, so for high engagement, we need different solutions.

I hear the term "Employee Experience" used often. Is that the same as employee engagement?

Employee experience includes all the workplace, employee policies and management practices that impact people on the job. If we look at the four scenarios above, whatever box you find yourself in, that is your "employee experience". Companies need to examine all employment and management practices so that both the satisfaction and the engagement factors are top class. People are looking to work for organisations where they experience a fulfilling, rewarding and enjoyable work experience, i.e. high engagement and high satisfaction. Companies therefore need to reflect on how their employees experience the workplace and ensure it leads to high engagement.

Is engagement just another term for workaholism?

Positive psychology researchers view engagement and workaholism as two different ways of experiencing work.[6] Whether you are engaged or a workaholic, you work hard but the experience differs. People who are highly engaged are in a positive state of "flow", enjoyment and enthusiasm, whereas workaholics tend to experience more negative energy in the form of feeling tense, driven, irritable and under pressure. Engagement is a good type of working hard, whereas workaholism can lead to burnout.

Can the impact of employee engagement on company performance be quantified?

One organisation that has measured the impact of engagement on company results is Gallup. Gallup researchers studied the differences in performance between engaged and actively disengaged work units, and found that those scoring in the top half on employee engagement nearly doubled their odds of success compared with those in the bottom half.[7]

Gallup's data reveals that business units in the top quartile of their global employee engagement database are 17% more productive and 21% more profitable than those in the bottom quartile.[8]

A research study into the impact of employee engagement on company performance based on 28 years of data was reported in the Harvard Business Review. The finding was that companies with high employee satisfaction and engagement outperform their peers by 2.3% to 3.8% per year in long-run stock returns. This adds up to an 89% to 184% cumulative increase. The data analysed were from the list of the 100 Best Companies to Work for in America, a well-respected survey where 250 workers are selected at random and questions covering credibility, respect, fairness, pride and camaraderie are asked of them. The research finding was that the benefits of employee satisfaction and engagement do outweigh the costs.[9]

How important is it to employees that they feel highly engaged at work?

So far, we have only looked at the benefits of high engagement to the leader and the company. Engagement at work is, however, also an important issue for the individual employee, as research shows it plays a significant role in a person's overall well-being and happiness.[10, 11]

People in a corporate environment generally work long hours, so to be happy at work is crucial for overall well-being. Many research studies have confirmed that loving your job is a key component of a person's individual happiness, life satisfaction, feelings of success and fulfilment, overall sense of well-being and even health.

> "Returning from work feeling inspired, safe, fulfilled and grateful is a natural human right to which we are all entitled and not a modern luxury that only a few lucky ones are able to find."
>
> — **Simon Sinek**, *Leaders Eat Last: Why Some Teams Pull Together and Others Don't*[12]

How does loving your work contribute to your well-being?

Our well-being and happiness are important as they set off an upward spiral of success in many aspects of life, in turn leading to more well-being and happiness.

> **TED**
> Ideas worth spreading
>
> Shawn Achor, in his TED Talk, The Happiness Advantage, shows us that happiness leads to success and not the other way around:
> https://www.ted.com/talks/shawn_achor_the_happy_secret_to_better_work

What do we mean by an upward spiral and how does well-being and happiness set this off?

When you feel good your brain generates happy chemicals like dopamine and serotonin, which

- increase your energy levels;
- improve your immune system;
- make you more resilient and optimistic;
- help you think more clearly;
- help you to be more creative;
- give you a greater capacity for learning and a willingness to take on new challenges; and
- may also improve your relationships.

Successfully dealing with challenges leads to more feelings of success and self-confidence, which energises you to take on new challenges, develop new skills, and experience more successes, confidence, optimism and greater well-being. This is the upward spiral. Feelings of success in all of these areas of life fuel greater levels of happiness and well-being.[13]

Figure 3: The Upward Spiral

Your well-being and happiness increase your chances of good outcomes and these good outcomes increase well-being and happiness.

Work and well-being

As an employee, if you love your work, you have something to look forward to every working day, yet we often think that work robs us of our enjoyment of life. Take a look at all the "Monday" jokes on the Internet. We usually think about work from the standpoint of all the things we have to do; the pressure, the uncertainty as companies merge or re-structure, budget cuts, difficult bosses, colleagues and customers. Many people do not believe that work and happiness go together. Their view is that work is something you do in order to be able to pursue happiness elsewhere. And if you want to be successful at work, happiness must be sacrificed.

But work can contribute to well-being and happiness at many levels. Let's look at work from the view of what it can do for the employee. Our first thoughts about work are usually, "I need to earn a living". Yes, we need to work to pay the bills, and as we become more successful at work, the more we earn, which has a direct influence on our standard of living. More money certainly opens up more opportunities and options in terms of where and how we live, the car we drive, the material goods we can buy, the holidays we can enjoy and so on. Money also buys us security in the form of savings, medical insurance, retirement policies etc.

However, there is more to work than just what we earn and what we do with it. There are more ways in which we can view work, so let's look at working at its best and all the additional ways in which work can contribute to our well-being.

Work also provides employees with a sense of community and belonging; we are part of a team – we have managers, supervisors, colleagues and customers with whom we interact on an ongoing basis. For many people, we see more of our work colleagues than we do of our families. When relationships at work are good, we form deep bonds with people and look forward to seeing them at work. We develop a shared history with these people; we often recall the pressures we faced together, the problems we resolved, the hilarious situations we encountered and the people we had to deal with, and there is often fun and laughter as we reminisce. We also look to these people for support when we are under pressure and our colleagues often provide a listening ear when we have personal problems or we are going through difficult times.

Work can also help us feel good about ourselves, firstly, through a sense of achievement. When we achieve tough targets or get that promotion, we feel successful. When people depend on us for a product or service, we feel a certain sense of importance and pride. Also, when we are recognised and acknowledged for work done well, we feel good about ourselves. Work can also provide us with status in our communities and families, depending on where we work, what we do and how successful we are perceived to be. All of these feed our self-esteem and self-confidence, which are essential for our well-being.

We develop as people by working; we develop the functional skills we need to do our daily work, and we gain experience and develop expertise as we are exposed to new and more complex challenges. We also develop skills such as people skills, problem solving skills, the ability to be creative and innovative, an understanding of our organisation's context and challenges, an understanding of our customers' needs, the ability to deal with stress and pressure, and many more. Many of the skills we develop are solely as a result of being at work: we grow in response to new challenges, opportunities and situations. Every new challenge stretches us a little further and we grow new skills and develop our personal qualities. Personal growth and realising our potential are strong needs in most people, and work certainly offers many opportunities for that.

Finally, work offers us the opportunity to use our talents and skills to make a positive difference in our world.

We are in our full power at work when our work aligns to our strengths and offers us an opportunity to make a difference to something that is important to us; something we are passionate about.

All of this is what work can potentially offer us; this is work at its best. Work offers us the opportunity to unlock our potential and achieve personal greatness, if we so choose.

How well are companies doing when it comes to employee engagement?

Now that we see the benefits of employee engagement to employees, leaders, companies, customers and shareholders, we may conclude that companies are working hard on the employee engagement issue, yet this does not seem to be the case. Most research suggests that organisations are not doing very well when it comes to employee engagement.[14] As we all know, not everyone finds themselves in a situation where they love their work and look forward to being at work. There are people who are underpaid, in uncomfortable or hostile environments, doing mundane work and feeling unfulfilled. Work can be a source of stress and for many people, work can break down their confidence and self-esteem rather than build it. Some people simply feel plateaued in their career and lacking in energy for the challenges ahead.

According to Gallup, a staggering 85% of employees worldwide are not engaged. This is a barrier to creating high-performing cultures and amounts to wasted potential. Many companies are experiencing a crisis of engagement and aren't aware of it.[15]

Glassdoor, a company that allows employees to rate their employers, reports that only 54% of employees recommend their company as a place to work.

In a recent survey among 80 of the most advanced users of engagement surveys, only half stated that their executives know how to build a culture of engagement. Among the broader population, the percentage is far lower.[16]

In the HR.com survey of HR professionals, only two-fifths said their senior leaders prioritise employee engagement, and just 28% said their managers are highly skilled at fostering engaged individuals and teams. In terms of discretionary effort or going the extra mile, only 9% strongly agreed that their employees do so. This indicates that most employers still face major employee engagement challenges.[17] The question for you as the leader or the HR leader in your company is: How do you prevent disengagement and how do you build teams of highly engaged people? Research carried out by Deloitte suggests that it is time for companies to focus on building "irresistible organizations".[18]

Researchers in the field of positive psychology have concluded that for people to be fully engaged with their work, intrinsic factors need to be addressed more strongly.[19] The most commonly mentioned are:

- company culture;
- inspiring leadership;
- work aligned to my strengths;
- work with meaning and purpose;
- a sense of achievement and contribution;
- autonomy;
- clarity regarding role and goals and an empowering performance review system;
- opportunities for learning and growth;
- recognition;
- a sense of belonging and a positive work climate;

- pride in the organisation; and
- a flexible work environment.

Focusing on these factors should give us good results in terms of employee engagement, however people are fascinating and unique and driven by their own ever-changing needs, so expect surprises, new insights and increased leadership wisdom as you work with these principles. Judgement is required in terms of how to implement inspiring leadership and employment practices. People differ so we need insight into them as individuals in order to find out what it is that lights them up at work and what fulfilment, success and happiness at work means to each person.

The chapters that follow will help you to think through your work situation and offer ways to enhance or make changes at work that will take you in the direction of:

- greater success, fulfilment, well-being and happiness if you are an individual employee;
- inspiring leadership practices that bring out the best in your employees if you are a leader; and
- employment policies and practices that contribute to high engagement if you are an HR leader.

Summary

In this chapter, I have outlined the case for making employee engagement a high priority in any organisation. For an organisation to be successful, an essential is to make people feel engaged with their work.

I have also unpacked the meaning of the terms "engagement", "satisfaction" and "employee experience", and we can see that "engagement" is largely influenced by intangible factors. It is also important to consider the impact of work on employees; work can contribute to a person's well-being in many ways. What I will address in the following chapters is the "how to" of employee engagement, which is aimed at leaders, HR leaders and individual employees. Briefly this is what I will cover in each chapter:

Chapter 2	The work climate for high engagement
Chapter 3	Strengths-based leadership
Chapter 4	How work can provide a sense of meaning, purpose and contribution
Chapter 5	Learning and development at work
Chapter 6	Leadership for high engagement
Chapter 7	Measuring employee engagement
Chapter 8	Organisational issues

We will be following Rochelle's progress with her team and in Chapter 8, Laurisha will reply to Daniel's outburst.

Please spend time on the reflective questions at the end of each chapter as clarity will emerge from these. It might be good to work through this book with a trusted friend or a coach and share your thoughts.

Reflective questions: Employees

Schaufeli, Bakker and Salanova developed a questionnaire to measure work engagement, the Utrecht Work Engagement Scale (UWES).[20] The questions that follow are based on their three aspects of engagement:

How engaged do you feel in your current job? (Rate yourself out of 10 on each of the following criteria.)

- Energy: do you have high levels of energy and resilience at work, are you willing to put in a great deal of effort, and do you persevere in the face of difficulties?

- Dedication: do you find the work that you do to be important and meaningful, do you feel proud of your job, do you feel a sense of responsibility, and do you feel inspired and challenged by your work?

- Flow: are you totally engrossed in your work and do you have difficulty tearing yourself away from it? (Time passes quickly and you forget everything else around you.)

Energy score ___ Dedication score ____ Flow score ___ Total score ___

What are your scores telling you?

If you are working currently, what impact is work having on your sense of well-being? What potential exists for a rich and interesting work life?

What is your definition of success at work? How successful do you feel currently?

What energises you at work? How often is this happening currently? When do you feel most fulfilled at work?

Reflective questions: Leaders

Looking at the signs of engagement and disengagement on page 9-11. What are you seeing mostly in your team/department/division/company?

What is your current approach to employee engagement and how well is it working?

Reflective questions: HR leaders

Is employee engagement one of the core business strategies in your company?

What does HR need to do to ensure informed discussion among top management on the topic of employee engagement?

Section 2

The Engagement Toolkit for leaders

> ### ❓ A question for senior and HR leaders
>
> Imagine you are a collector of Koi and you import beautiful fish from Japan that cost a fortune. Would you put them in dirty, murky water? Of course not; you would make sure everything in their environment was as perfect as you could get it so their brilliance shines through.
>
> Yet how often do we do this to our talented employees? We do this when we place people in areas of the company where the environment is toxic due to poor leadership and expect them to shine. And worse, when they do not perform to the level we expect, we blame the person instead of addressing the situation.

In this next section, we follow Rochelle's development as a leader as she works with her coach to gain a better understanding of the drivers of employee engagement.

We will look at the following drivers of employee engagement:

- The organisational climate required for high engagement.
- Work that is aligned to one's strengths.
- Work with meaning and purpose.
- Personal and work-related growth and development.
- Leadership roles and styles.

As people move beyond survival needs at work, these issues become important to their engagement at work.

Individual employees also have a role to play in their engagement at work; they need good self-insight regarding their strengths and personal values so they can make good career choices.

As a leader, I need a good understanding of these drivers of engagement so I can set people up to make their greatest contributions at work and grow their skills, which in turn contributes to the company's success.

Our engagement at work is therefore both a personal responsibility as well as a leadership responsibility.

Figure 4: Model for Employee Engagement

Chapter 2

The work climate for engagement

> In this chapter we look at the important topic of psychological safety and how leaders can help create it.

"And when a leader embraces their responsibility to care for people instead of caring for numbers, then people will follow, solve problems and see to it that that leader's vision comes to life the right way, a stable way and not the expedient way."

— **Simon Sinek,** *Leaders Eat Last: Why Some Teams Pull Together and Others Don't*

> See these YouTube videos by Simon Sinek who shares why a circle of safety is an essential element to organisational leadership – https://www.youtube.com/watch?v=LOnXcrmgAw8
>
> He explains in this video why good leaders make you feel safe and suggests it's someone who makes their employees feel secure, and draws them into a circle of trust – https://www.youtube.com/watch?v=lmyZMtPVodo

Rochelle gets a coach

Rochelle was fed up with her team. The energy and innovation she expected from them was just not there. Through the company's coaching programme, she selected Nicholas to be her coach.

At her first coaching session, Rochelle vented her feelings about her team. "I am so frustrated with them", she told Nicholas. "I expected so much from this team but they are just not stepping up."

"Tell me what you expected", said Nicholas.

"As a marketing team, we need innovative ideas", said Rochelle. "I expect that my people will say what they think, put ideas forward, speak their minds and give candid feedback. I need them to be more creative and innovative and see more possibilities. It's OK to share half-formed ideas. And let's take some risks; if people try something and it hasn't worked, let's hear about it so we can all learn from it. I want people to feel free to bounce ideas off each other, express their concerns, make suggestions, help solve problems and provide support to each other.

"Also, if people don't know something, I want them to ask questions and be OK to admit that they don't know or don't understand something. It's the only way we will learn and come up with innovative ideas. I also want people to be willing to take ownership of projects to address needs and opportunities."

"And what is happening in your team?", asked Nicholas. Rochelle sighed. "Almost the opposite. It seems to me people stay quiet unless they are sure that what they have to say fits with my thinking. They wait until they can see where my thinking is going before they say anything. No-one will talk about a mistake, and I think problems are hidden. There seems to be a fear of reprisal and victimisation. I hear people saying things like, 'It would be career-limiting to say that'. I also don't like the 'blame game' that happens; rather than taking responsibility for errors or delays on our side, we blame other departments. When my boss is around, everyone agrees with him even when it's not a very good idea. There seems to be a pattern of not wanting to look incompetent, so they don't say they don't know and they don't want to fail so we don't try something new. Also, we avoid taking ownership of a project or problem to be solved in case it does not go well and there is some type of 'punishment' or loss of reputation.

"How do I break these patterns?"

Psychological safety is the foundation for employee engagement

If we want people to be at their best at work, we first need to attend to the climate in which people work.

Creating an engaging work climate can be daunting for leaders if our attention is mainly on chasing the results. However, leaders can encourage behaviours in the team that set the tone for the right workplace climate and lay the foundation for high engagement.

Recent research is helping us to better understand the conditions required for people to be fully engaged at work. One important study was undertaken by Google, which collected large amounts of data in order to try to better understand its people and to find out why some teams at Google excelled while others did not.[21]

They expected to find that if you want to build the most successful teams, all you need to do is bring in the best people, yet this was not the conclusion they came to. Ultimately they came up with a list of the five key dynamics required for team success:

Psychological safety: Psychological safety refers to an individual's perception that a team is safe for risk taking and they will not be labelled as ignorant, incompetent, negative, or disruptive. Team members feel confident that no one on the team will embarrass or punish those who make a mistake, ask a question, or offer a new idea.

Dependability: In dependable teams, members can be relied on to do quality work on time and will not shirk responsibilities.

Structure and clarity: An individual understands the job expectations, how to fulfil these, and the importance of their role for team effectiveness.

Meaning: Finding a sense of purpose in either the work itself or the output is important for team effectiveness. The meaning of work is personal and can vary from financial security to supporting family, helping the team succeed, or self-expression.

Impact: The results of one's work and the belief that your work is making a difference and contributing to the organisation's goals.

While all five were needed to create a successful team, **psychological safety** stood out as the most important factor. Since then, research has shown that psychological safety can make not just teams, but entire organisations, perform better.

According to Harvard Business School professor Amy Edmondson, psychological safety refers to "a shared belief that the team is safe for interpersonal risk taking". In other words, there is high trust and a belief that you won't be punished when you make a mistake, or humiliated for speaking up with ideas, questions or concerns.[22, 23]

TED
Ideas worth spreading

For inspiration see Professor Amy Edmondson's TED Talk on "Building a psychologically safe workplace".

People are at their best when they are in a work climate where they feel "safe". Simon Sinek calls this a "Circle of Safety", which is an environment of trust, respect and cooperation where people can be authentic and thrive.[24]

For this to happen it is essential that leaders create safe and respectful workplaces, where someone "has my back".

Some leaders try to "motivate" people through fear, but as soon as we feel fear, engagement levels suffer and we end up with mediocre performance. We all want to do well, make a contribution, be successful and be respected. As soon as we feel the need to protect ourselves from being judged, humiliated, excluded or embarrassed, or we have fears about our careers and reputation, we may find ourselves getting into destructive and protective behaviours which break down trust and psychological safety. If we work in a low trust fear culture, then we get into the behaviour patterns Rochelle describes in her team.

> A manager described project meetings as "prayer meetings". As soon as ideas were asked for, everyone's head dropped, hoping someone else would say something!

Psychological safety creates positive emotions like trust, belonging, respect, confidence and creativity. We can be vulnerable, say we don't know, talk about our failures and feel supported. These emotions broaden the mind and help us to find solutions to complex problems, enabling us to become more courageous, resilient and engaged.

Improving psychological safety starts with leadership. Team members are particularly aware of the behaviour of the leader; how the leader responds to events influences their perceptions of what is an appropriate and "safe" way to behave.

The concept of psychological safety is supported by neuroscience; when we don't feel safe, we are not at our best. Here is a brief summary from the work of David Rock describing what happens to us when we don't feel safe:[25]

Your brain at work; some key insights:

- One of the key functions of the brain is to keep us safe by scanning the environment for any threat to our safety.

- The brain quickly classifies things around us into things that will either "hurt" us or be "rewarding" to us. This leads to either "move away" behaviour or "move toward" behaviour.

- The brain does not distinguish between a physical threat (e.g. someone is about to attack me) and a social threat (e.g. I am about to be humiliated or criticised).

- The brain, more specifically the amygdala, which is part of the limbic system, reacts in the same way to a physical and a social threat, which is to pump adrenaline and cortisol into our systems, making us physically stronger. We then go into fight, flight or freeze mode as a way to protect ourselves.

- The amygdala fires up more intensely when it senses a threat compared to when it senses a reward; the reaction comes on much faster, lasts a lot longer and is more difficult to recover from.

- On the other hand, the "toward/reward" sensation is a lot more subtle and very easily displaced. This explains why the reaction to criticism lasts a lot longer and has a greater impact than praise.

- When we are stressed or fearful, energy is drained away from the thinking part of our brain, which is the prefrontal cortex. This means we are less able to memorise, reason, be creative, answer questions, develop new insights, make decisions and understand information. We also tend to only see problems and are less willing to take risks; we tend to think things cannot be done because we are less able to see solutions.

- Unfortunately, it is very easy to fire up the limbic system into a stress response and once that happens, it can set off a downward spiral of events. Think, for example, of giving a presentation to a critical audience. Because you are stressed, you don't present confidently and clearly and you don't handle tough questions well, which makes you more stressed. Counter-proposals are made which you respond to negatively, which makes the audience hostile and so it goes on.

- If you are repeatedly in an environment where you do not feel safe, your cortisol and adrenaline levels remain high. You now experience a permanent sense of threat and anxiety. The high levels of adrenaline and cortisol affect your physical health as well as your memory, creativity and reasoning, all of which are essential to your success at work.

- To be fully engaged at work, you need to feel you are in a safe space. Then the brain signals it is safe to move "towards" situations. Abilities such as creativity, reasoning, curiosity, memory and insight come to the fore. These are the brain states associated with high engagement and success at work.

- When we feel safe and trusting, our brain generates "feel-good" chemicals such as dopamine, serotonin and oxytocin. This makes us feel more positive, closer to others and more energised.

- At work, trust and purpose release oxytocin which produces happiness and high engagement levels.

- To feel psychological safety is clearly not just a "nice-to-have". It is essential for success and well-being, as well as for healthy working relationships of support, collaboration and innovation.

The Energy Matrix[26, 27]

The Energy Matrix helps you to assess the climate in your team:

- The vertical axis runs from LOW ENERGY to HIGH ENERGY. Energy includes a person's mental, emotional and physical energy at work.

- The horizontal axis runs from NEGATIVE ENERGY to POSITIVE ENERGY. When people at work are positive, confident, optimistic and engaged, we see positive energy. We achieve positive energy among people when they have a sense of psychological safety. When people are stressed, anxious, irritable or frustrated, we see negative energy in action.

Four scenarios then emerge, as per the diagram below:

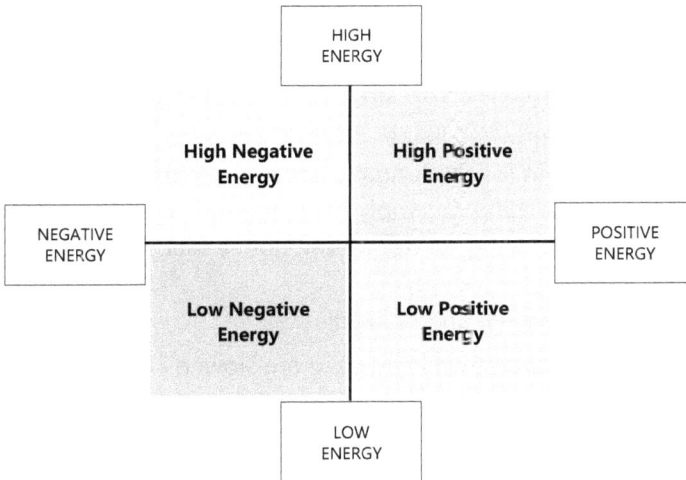

```
                        HIGH
                        ENERGY

          High Negative        High Positive
            Energy               Energy

 NEGATIVE                                      POSITIVE
 ENERGY                                        ENERGY

          Low Negative         Low Positive
            Energy               Energy

                         LOW
                        ENERGY
```

Figure 5: The Energy Matrix

The 4 Energy Quadrants

1. **High positive energy:** This describes people who feel "safe", who are highly engaged with their work, who are supportive of their company's goals, and who are in trusting and supportive relationships with their colleagues and managers. As leaders it

is the climate we should strive to achieve in our organisations. When people are in the high positive energy quadrant, we see high engagement, including:

■ effort and perseverance;

■ contribution;

■ people feel they can be authentic and speak their truth;

■ creativity and innovation;

■ a willingness to collaborate and support others;

■ a commitment to quality and a great customer experience; and

■ people trust that their leaders have their best interests at heart.

2. **Low positive energy:** This describes people who are complacent. Realistically, people do need a recovery time from high levels of energy and effort, and we all spend some time in this quadrant. As a leader it is not a quadrant we want our people to be in for too long, however it is a good time for reflection, coaching or simply "catching up". When people are in a low positive energy state, we will notice that:

■ they look calm and relaxed;

■ their reaction times and pace are slower;

■ trust, peace and harmony reigns;

■ they are content;

■ relationships are good; and

■ there is a relaxed "vibe".

3. **High negative energy:** We all have days when things go wrong and we feel frustrated and irritable, but this energy is destructive if it becomes the norm. When people are in the high negative energy quadrant, we will notice that:

■ they are tense, anxious and irritable;

■ there is aggressive behaviour;

- conflict erupts easily and quickly, i.e. they are easily triggered;
- resistance to change is high as any change looks like a new threat;
- they are competitive and want to "win" at all costs;
- internal politics are rife and people are advised to "watch their backs"; and
- trust levels are low.

4. **Low negative energy:** This is the most difficult quadrant to manage as energy is both negative and low. This is the state of 'giving up'. When people are in the low negative energy quadrant we notice that they are:

- cynical and sceptical;
- distrustful of their leadership and colleagues;
- withdrawn;
- more likely to dismiss company information and rely on rumours;
- unwilling to take on a challenge or a new project; and
- fearful.

tips/ideas

Look again at the descriptions above of the four energy matrix quadrants. In your team or organsation, what is the predominant mood?

What are the implications of this for leadership?

To create a culture of high, positive energy. we need to encourage some specific behaviours in the team and of course we need to be the role model for whatever it is we are asking others to do.

- Creating **high** energy requires a compelling vision or an interesting challenge (more about that in Chapter 4).
- Building **positive** energy requires people to work together to create psychological safety.

Important actions a leader must take to create positive energy and psychological safety

Psychological safety begins when I have a great relationship with my manager and my colleagues. For this to happen, we all need to work on trustful, respectful and collaborative relationships, with the leader leading the way. When we have this kind of connection with people at work, we feel more valued, competent and engaged.

> "We are hardwired to connect with others; it's what gives purpose and meaning to our lives, and without it there is suffering."
>
> — **Brené Brown**, *Daring Greatly: How the Courage to Be Vulnerable Transforms the Way We Live, Love, Parent, and Lead*[28]

1. Build trust in the team

Building a climate of high trust is the foundation for psychological safety. Employees in high-trust organisations are more productive, have more energy at work, collaborate better with their colleagues, feel a lot calmer, and tend to stay with their employers longer than people working at low-trust companies. They also suffer less chronic stress and are happier with their lives, and these factors fuel stronger performances. In a low-trust environment, people tend to withdraw and not communicate openly as their focus is on protecting themselves.

Compared with people at low-trust companies, people at high-trust companies report 74% less stress, 106% more energy at work, 50% higher productivity, 13% fewer sick days, 76% more engagement, 29% more satisfaction with their lives, and 40% less burnout. When we feel safe our brain generates dopamine and serotonin, which makes us feel positive and optimistic, as well as oxytocin, which makes us feel closer to others.[29]

In a high-trust environment, less energy is wasted on wondering if someone is telling you the truth or if there is a hidden agenda. We can move forward a lot quicker when we trust people.

> "A team is not a group of people that work together. A team is a group of people that trust each other."
>
> **— Simon Sinek**[30]

As the leader, we need to encourage people to be more honest, courageous and authentic by speaking more openly, opening up the tough issues for discussion, highlighting problems, resolving our conflicts and disagreements, and supporting others. We should not have a situation where there is polite agreement in meetings and dissension in private afterwards.

Stephen Covey, in his book The Seven Habits of Highly Effective People, describes the importance of trust in relationships. He uses the metaphor of an emotional bank account.

"We all know what a financial bank account is. We make deposits into it and build up a balance from which we can make withdrawals when we need to. An Emotional Bank Account describes the amount of trust that's been built up in a relationship. It's the feeling of safeness you have with another human being.

"If I make deposits into an Emotional Bank Account with you through courtesy, kindness, honesty and keeping my commitments to you, I build up a balance. Your trust towards me becomes higher, and I can call upon that trust many times if I need to. I can even make mistakes and that trust level, that emotional balance, will compensate for it. My communication may not be clear, but you'll get my meaning anyway. You won't make me "an offender for a word." When the trust account is high, communication is easy, instant, and effective.

"But if I have a habit of showing discourtesy, disrespect, not keeping my commitments, cutting you off, overreacting, ignoring you, betraying your trust, threatening you, or being a dictator, eventually my Emotional Bank Account is overdrawn. The trust level gets very low. Then what flexibility do I have?

"None. I'm walking on mine fields. I have to be very careful of everything I say. I measure every word. It's tension city, memo haven. It's protecting my backside, politicking. And many organisations are filled with it. Many families are filled with it. Many marriages are filled with it".

Below is a list of behaviours that build trust. As a leader we should hold ourselves accountable for these behaviours first, and then encourage team members to do the same.[31]

Trust building behaviours include:

- courtesy;
- kindness;
- empathy;
- fairness;
- mostly a "win-win" approach to resolving problems;
- honesty and openness, sharing of information, ideas and feelings;
- a concern for others' needs as well as your own;
- listening to understand and acknowledging others' views;
- a willingness to accept feedback and constructive criticism;
- admitting when you are wrong;
- integrity (adopting good principles and living according to them);
- seeing the good in others;
- supporting others' good ideas;
- keeping your commitments;
- being reliable and dependable;

- being consistent (you walk your talk and set a good example);
- being willing to share experience and knowledge with others;
- giving assistance when required;
- accepting and respecting other people, even when there are differences in values, cultures and personalities;
- consulting people before making decisions which affect them; and
- showing good judgement and having the competence and skills to contribute to the work of this group. People want to work with leaders and team members who are skilled and knowledgeable about the technical aspects of the job and who have a depth of experience.

tips/ideas

Consider sharing this list with your team and asking people to reflect on what they as individuals are putting into the team's "trust account".

2. Build a climate of respect

When co-workers engage with each other respectfully, people experience a greater sense of self-worth and competence. Respectful engagement empowers and energises, giving individuals a heightened sense of their abilities.[32]

Respect is an important part of building trust, and being trustworthy also builds respect.

Nancy Kline described a Thinking Environment, which is a set of principles that builds psychological safety and an environment of respect which allows us to be at our best and do our best thinking. Her components of a Thinking Environment include:[33]

- listening to each other with our full attention and without interrupting. This includes switching off our phones and focusing on the other person;

- ensuring all voices are heard. This means in meetings, the more talkative people discipline themselves to keep it short and concise and remember to draw in the quieter people. Introverts are often overlooked in meetings and in many cases, have great insights to share. Make sure everyone is invited to contribute their ideas;

- a sense of ease and not being rushed. Being interrupted and rushed generates adrenaline which reduces the quality of our thinking. We need to listen and allow people to finish speaking;

- an appreciation of each other's contributions to the team. We need to affirm each other and acknowledge their strengths and contribution to the team. We must not allow sarcasm or personal attacks;

- being comfortable with emotions and allowing people to feel their feelings. This includes encouraging laughter, as this helps to generate dopamine and serotonin which helps the quality of our thinking;

- sharing information and facing the facts. Encourage people to speak their truth and to be open to others' points of view. Encourage rigorous and clear thinking without creating defensiveness;

- appreciating diversity. To generate our best thinking we need to welcome diverse points of view and let people know it is OK to think differently, as this is where cutting edge ideas may emerge. In fact, encourage out of the box and off the wall suggestions, as they often lead to the most innovative ideas;

- collaboration and support rather than competition. This builds trust and respect and helps us do our best thinking without feeling threatened;

- open questions. These expand our thinking and challenge our assumptions and help us make the best decisions; and

■ physical work environment also signals respect so make sure offices and meeting rooms are functional and comfortable.

tips/ideas

At the end of a team coaching session with a team where there had been lots of conflict, they decided at the end of monthly meetings to have an "Appreciation Round". Each team member mentioned something they appreciated about other team members, e.g. something they had done well, assistance they had given, or a personal quality they admired about another person.

3. **Encourage collaboration, support and co-creating conversations**

Many problems and challenges require input from multiple sources, such as other functions, teams within the company, and maybe even customers and suppliers.

To collaborate successfully, leaders must be able to communicate clearly, be excellent listeners, and manage differences of opinions and competing agendas.

For this reason, leaders need to know how to have co-creating conversations. In *Conversational Intelligence*, Judith Glaser describes three types of conversations:[34]

■ In Level 1 conversations we simply exchange information.

■ In Level 2 conversations we try to persuade others to come around to our point of view and we are not open to the views of others.

■ In Level 3 conversations we co-create by sharing our views, listening, exploring and building on each other's ideas. We listen to connect, not judge or criticise, and we ask questions for which we have no answers so we explore and discover new ideas.

These conversations can lead to outcomes better than we ever imagined.[35]

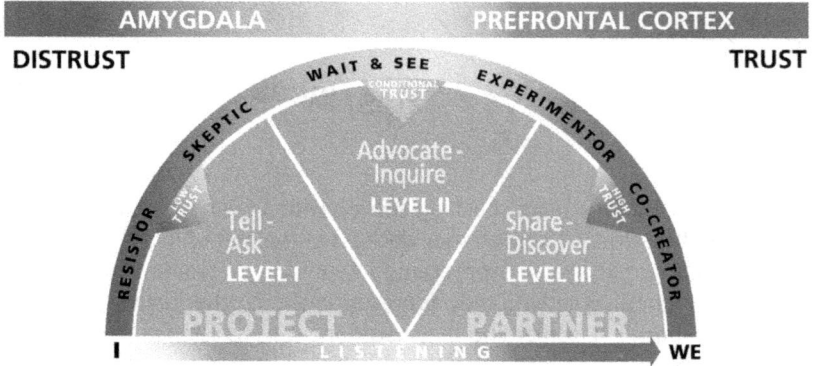

Figure 6: Conversational dashboard™ [36]

4. **Help team members prevent or resolve conflicts**

We all have our bad days and do things that upset others. We will have disagreements. If we feel we have been treated badly in some way, we may resort to criticism, competition or disengagement out of anger or frustration, all of which creates a bad atmosphere at work. Conflict is normal and expected. The main thing for the leader is to ensure that conflicts are resolved quickly and effectively, as if left unresolved, they will create a tense environment and cause a break down in trust.

As the leader we need to help people repair their relationships. We must support our teams to become comfortable enough to work through a conflict and give and receive feedback from each other.

Behaviours which typically cause conflict and break down trust include:

- discourtesy, rudeness or aggression;
- disrespect;
- self-centredness (a "win-lose" approach);

- not keeping commitments (being unreliable);
- being manipulative or having hidden agendas;
- being unkind;
- arrogance;
- taking all the credit;
- putting people down (focussing on their faults only);
- cutting people off;
- overreacting;
- ignoring people;
- making arbitrary decisions;
- betraying someone's trust;
- threatening; and
- being dictatorial.[37]

In any conflict situation we must be aware of assumptions we are making about the other person's behaviour and their intentions behind it. Judith Glaser describes this as the Ladder of Conclusions:[38]

- Something happens, e.g. a team member does not give me an important piece of information.

- There is a consequence for me: I make a wrong decision and my boss gets a call from a furious customer.

- I come to a conclusion about why that happened, e.g. my team member is inconsiderate or is trying to undermine me or make me look incompetent or setting me up for failure.

- The incident, but mainly my conclusion about why it happened, leads me to feel angry and humiliated, and there is an outburst in the office which everyone hears. The atmosphere is tense and the conflict is unresolved, meaning it is time for the leader to step up and resolve the conflict.

How to resolve conflicts

When tensions are running high between two people, you may need to get them together and work through a conflict-resolution process.

- Ask the person with the problem to describe the situation: what happened and what the consequences were. Do not allow any interruptions.

- Ask the person how he/she interpreted the behaviour, or the assumptions he/she came to, i.e. when you did... or when this happened... it seemed to me, or I thought you were...

- Ask the other person to respond:

- What happened and why did it happen that way?

- Regarding the conclusions the other person came to, if they don't agree with the conclusion, they may acknowledge that they can see how the person came to that conclusion, e.g. "My intention was never to undermine you, but I can see how it might look that way".

- Ask both parties what is needed now to fix the situation and how we can move forward.

- Summarise who will do what and thank both parties for engaging in the conversation.

5. **Recognise excellence**

Many employees feel taken for granted and not valued at work, even when they have achieved something really great. Over time this erodes engagement as people feel that they should not bother if their efforts are not valued or appreciated.

Genuine appreciation and recognition plays a big role in creating positive energy. Recognition can be both personal and public, and should be given as soon after the achievement as possible. Public recognition may also inspire others to achieve.

The person receiving the recognition feels great as their self-esteem and confidence are boosted. They get a rush of dopamine and serotonin which makes them want to repeat this good experience, and they feel energised to maintain their efforts.

As the leader we need to focus on what is going right as well as on the problems, and express our appreciation – a short note to the employee, a public thank you at the next team meeting, or highlighting the success to your management will boost positive energy at work.

Your company may have a formal recognition scheme and maybe you let the person or team know that you will be nominating them for an award.

A best practice example

Volkswagen Group South Africa has an employee recognition programme where employees nominate teams who have achieved extraordinary results in various parts of the business. For example, these include achievements in the areas of production and marketing, as well as any special achievements. A panel of judges selects the winners and runners up in each category. All nominees are recognised in the company newspaper. A black tie event takes place annually to formally acknowledge the winning teams.

6. Build relationships of belonging and inclusion, and an appreciation of diversity

Think back to a time when you felt "different". If you also felt excluded it would not have been a great experience. A sense of belonging, connection and inclusion is an important part of psychological safety. Our sense of engagement at work increases when we have good relationships, whether with a supervisor, colleagues, or customers.

Work teams are becoming more diverse, which is an advantage if we handle it well as this gives us access to a wider range of experiences, thinking and ideas. This is great for innovation and creative problem solving. Leaders are now having to manage people across generations (including team members who may be their parents' ages) from different functions, who may know more than he/she does about certain topics, as well as people with different backgrounds, mindsets and value systems.

The leader's role is to create the conditions for everyone to operate at their best. This includes making sure everyone feels heard and included, that employees get along well, and that we welcome a diversity of thinking. It is always good to remind people that they each bring a unique perspective to the team as a result of their backgrounds, experiences and education. For example: "Aneesha, you worked in the Finance Division, could they make a decision based on this information we are giving them?"

Good relationships develop when there are more positive interactions than negative ones; a compliment on work well done, a word of support after a setback, a thank you for helping out, taking a personal interest in each other, and providing more encouragement and less criticism all add up to how we feel on the job.

A study of the highest performing teams on profitability, customer satisfaction and 360 degree evaluations found that they all experienced positive communication, personal connection and cohesion among team members. High quality connections at work lead to more learning, resilience, cooperation, job satisfaction and engagement.[39]

In any team environment, enjoyment and positivity arise from a combination of harmony, impact, and acknowledgment, all of which business leaders can engender in their organisations:

- **Harmony:** On winning teams, each player has a distinct role in achieving the goal. When the diverse skills and strengths of teammates are really clicking together, it feels great.
- **Impact:** Team harmony leads to impact, which further fuels joy.
- **Acknowledgment:** Great coaches instruct their players to, when they score, immediately point to the teammates who created the scoring opportunity. Acknowledging each player's contributions

and cheering for each other powers the entire joy-success-joy cycle.

Business leaders can provide people with more of the experiences that bring positivity and joy in any team setting, and thereby increase success and engagement.[40]

7. **Share information**

For a team to work well, they need information; good decisions cannot be made with incomplete information. Your job as a leader is to ensure that the team gets the information it needs. Information should flow as freely as possible and preferably not be withheld from certain people or certain levels of employees.

Bad communication is often quoted as a reason for all sorts of problems in organisations. Uncertainty and rumours also lead to stress, negativity and disengagement, and many employees feel they are not well-informed about their companies' strategies and actual performance. Sharing information on an ongoing basis is the solution to reducing this kind of stress.

Luckily, communication and information sharing is something that can be easily remedied – all it requires is for you to be proactive and to start the process of sharing or asking for information. This can be done by setting up regular meetings, asking for or sending out regular reports, or simply via informal networking. You can start to change the "lack of communication" problem in your organisation.

The diagram below highlights the information that should be flowing from your team as well as into your team. Work with your team to evaluate what meetings are needed, who should attend each one, and what should be on the agenda. Make changes as required. Do the same with sending out reports and communiques via e-mail.

What information do we require from our leadership and each other?

■ How and when should this be shared?

■ What forums and meetings do we need?

What information should we be passing onto our leadership and each other?

■ How and when should this be conveyed?

Work Team

What information do we require from other teams or individuals?

■ For example, other departments, customers or suppliers.

What other teams depend on us for information?

■ How do we ensure this happens?

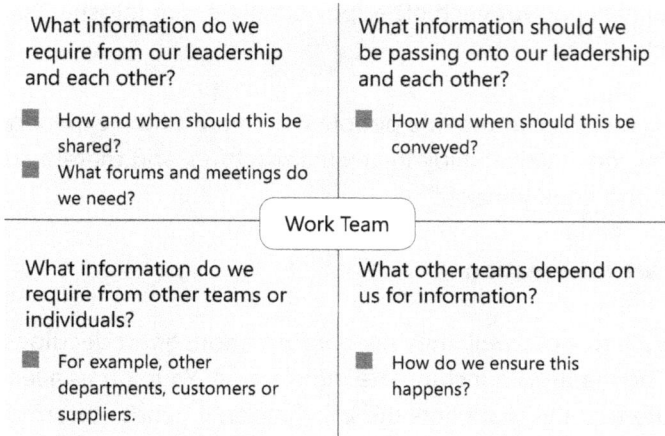

Figure 7: Information flows to and from your team

Be strategic in terms of meetings – most people's calendars are too full anyway, so think through who you invite to your meetings and which meetings you attend. Consider sending a team member to represent you at certain meetings; the exposure and information gained can be a great experience for a team member. However, ensure the person leading the meeting knows you will be sending a replacement and that the person you send is fully briefed and has some decision-making power. People leading meetings get very frustrated when a replacement arrives looking flustered and unsure what the meeting is all about, and then refuses to make any decisions affecting his or her department because they are not sure if they are allowed to.

Also be selective when it comes to sending out reports, as the approach of sending an e-mail to a few people and copying the rest of the company, flooding mailboxes and leading to information overload, does cause irritation.

Think through what you are currently doing in terms of communicating and what changes you can make to keep people informed but not overloaded with meetings and e-mails.

8. **Support people through change**

An engagement dilemma for leaders is that most organisations operate in a very dynamic environment and are going through rapid changes as technology and markets change. Companies need new products and services, as well as innovation in functional processes, and are adopting Agile methodologies across the organisation to achieve this. However, people generally prefer certainty and the known and dislike change. Just mention the word "restructure" or "new system", for example, and watch panic set in and rumours start.

Information, empathy and support help us to cope better with change and leaders need to help employees work through their resistance and accept the change.

I identified five 'F' words that describe how people respond to change. As leaders we need to accept that people may resist proposed changes and may get very angry or leave, and that it will take time to achieve buy-in. During any change, information is key; people want accurate information from their manager to either confirm or deny the rumours. Integrity is very important – if you are not permitted to say, then tell people; if it is still under discussion, let people know the status, but share whatever information you can.

FRIGHT and FREEZE When people first hear about a proposed change such as a restructure or a new work process, they may "freeze" and go into denial. They may deny that the change will happen or that it will continue or last. People in the denial stage are trying to avoid dealing with the fear and uncertainty of the change. The denial stage is difficult because it is hard to involve people in planning for the future when they will not acknowledge that the future is going to be any different than the present. People tend to move out of the denial stage when they see clear indicators that things will be different. Information is key!	
FIGHT or FLEE When people can see that change will happen, they may move into a state of anger and resistance. Some employees may choose to leave. They may be angry with their leadership for allowing this to happen to them. It is critical that leaders deal with this anger well and help people work through it so they can move to the next stage. If leadership is poor, the anger at this stage may last a long time.	
FLOW This is the stage where people begin to accept the change. They have a better understanding of the change and are more willing to explore it. They act more open-mindedly and are now more interested in planning around the change and being participants in the process. You may hear people saying, "We must just make the best of it". They can see it is a reality and have come to terms with it sufficiently to help make it work. While some changes will never get support (downsizing, for example), employees at this stage are willing to move forward and work within the new set up.	

Figure 8: Reactions to Change

9. **Encourage learning from failure**[41]

To create psychological safety, leaders have to accept that failures and mistakes will happen and deal with these in an appropriate way.

The interesting thing is that Amy Edmonson and Google both found that teams which made more mistakes were actually more successful.[42, 43] Creating an environment in which people feel safe to take some risks is essential for innovation; no tolerance for mistakes, no innovation. As leaders we have to encourage people to be open and disclose mistakes and failures, as well as the insights we can all learn from them.

Psychological safety means people will not be punished for small mistakes or asking for help. As leaders, we need to encourage the team to ask for help, clarifications, feedback or information.

People also need to accept that their ideas or suggestions may not work out or they may not be able to convince their team, but as the leader you can still encourage new ideas and experimentation.

Yet a tolerance for failure does not mean "anything goes" and that there are no consequences for poor performance; employees are still accountable for results and professional conduct. As leaders we need to both reward excellence and address poor performance, accepting that people will make errors and exercise poor judgement on occasions.

Blaming people makes them defensive and unwilling to explore what went wrong and learn from mistakes or things that went wrong. There are different types of errors and mistakes and each one needs a different approach:

- 'Errors' made as a result of trying out a new approach or process. These are valuable learning experiences and need to be shared so other people do not waste time trying the same approach. Punishing people for trying something new and not succeeding will stifle further attempts at innovation, however innovation needs to be managed so errors are not too costly. An employee should share their idea with the team and get their input first, and the experiment should be on a small scale. After the experiment or prototype, there should be a debriefing so learnings can be identified and a decision made regarding whether to change the idea, expand it or close it down.

■ For errors caused by process problems, overloading, high complexity or unexpected situations, a different approach is needed, i.e. there needs to be a conversation with the employee regarding the cause of the error. Is the person over-loaded or under some personal stress? Is this a new function the person has taken on and inexperience is the problem? Were there unusual circumstances? In these conversations, the focus is on finding the root cause and agreeing on ways to prevent problems in the future.

■ Errors due to carelessness or deliberately not following the process require the normal disciplinary process to be followed.

Neutralise fears people have about discussing anything that has gone wrong by stating your intention of trying to understand what happened and what we can learn from it, rather than blaming and punishing. In that way we create a learning culture rather than a fear culture.

10. **Allow people discretion and flexibility in how they do their work**

If you are confident that your employees have the necessary skills, allow them to do the work in their own way. As a leader, you cannot do everything yourself. Being trusted is a big motivator, while micro-management is a huge demotivator. With a less-experienced employee, encourage more frequent check-ins and ask more questions. With all employees, agree up-front on when you need feedback and updates. It takes courage for a leader to let go and allow others to make decisions, as we fear the consequences of possible mistakes. It is thus important that people understand when they need to check in with their managers.

Autonomy may also encourage innovation and new approaches to tasks. If you become aware of innovative approaches leading to great results, ask the employees concerned to give feedback to the rest of the team so that everyone can learn from and build on their successes. It is also a way of recognising the innovators.

Flexibility is important to employees and plays a role in employee loyalty. Employees increasingly do not want to be tied to strict hours or locations, and they also value the trust that their employers demonstrate in granting flexibility. According to the *Deloitte Millennial Survey,* Millennials believe that employers who are offering more flexibility than they did three years ago are also achieving greater profitability and providing work environments that are more stimulating, healthy and satisfying. However, not all employees are allowed flexible work arrangements; senior management teams have reported increased flexibility in where and when they work, but fewer respondents in more junior roles are enjoying flexible work arrangements.[44]

Ultimately, empowered teams are more productive, proactive and engaged.[45]

11. **Be accessible**

Being accessible is vital to building a psychologically safe environment. People feel more supported if they can easily talk to their leaders when they encounter problems. It may only take a few minutes to explain something or work something out together. It is also important that contact with a leader is positive and supportive and that employees are not made to feel stupid for not knowing how to proceed. Good leaders are approachable and encourage people to ask questions.

Employee engagement increases when people are able to see their manager at short notice to tell him or her what they need or what's on their mind and to receive immediate feedback. Employees appreciate their manager supporting them with work challenges as well as taking an interest in them as people. Psychological safety increases when people experience their leaders as open and approachable, and believe that they care about them as people.

12. **Bring more positivity and enjoyment into the workplace**

Success sparks joy. Joy fuels further success.[46]

Why is positivity important? Sean Achor described research that shows that when we are in a negative mindset, all challenges seem more difficult.[47]

To build positivity, we need to acknowledge successes, appreciate people and express gratitude for their efforts. Further, we need to acknowledge problems but also expand our view to see opportunities.

Finding the positive: Sindile was very despondent about her boss. In her coaching she described him as aggressive, challenging and unsupportive. He challenged every proposal she made and tried to find flaws in her approach. Discussions were generally robust and argumentative as he talked over her and she always left his office feeling worn down and wondering why she bothered.

Later on I asked her if she could see any benefits to her from his approach. After a long pause, she said, "By the time I get to the meetings where I need to present my proposals, I know that all the problem areas in my presentation have been sorted out and I am very prepared for anything that may come up. I definitely go in with a better presentation and more confidence."

I asked her if she could possibly view him as a supporter who is enhancing her reputation, and not her enemy. Sindile was taken aback by that suggestion, but a month later, she reported that she had been trying to view his behaviour through a different lens; she listened more instead of arguing, and her stress levels and negativity had dropped considerably.

In real life... an interview with Richard Branson

What are your top three leadership principles?

Branson: 1. Listening is one of the most important skills that anyone can have. That's a very Virgin trait. Listening enables us to learn from each other, from the marketplace, and from the mistakes that must be made in order to get anywhere that is original and disruptive. I learn so much from guests and employees that way.

2. Learn: Learning and leadership go together. Too much credit goes to me for what we have achieved at Virgin but the successes happen from working and learning with some of the world's most inspiring and inspired people.

3. Laughter: My number one rule in business, and in life, is to enjoy what you do. Running a business involves long hours and hard decisions; if you don't have the passion to keep you going, your business will more than likely fail. If you don't enjoy what you are doing, then you shouldn't be doing it.[48]

David Rock has identified five factors that the brain treats the same as survival issues. A threat to any of these triggers the "protect" response and floods our systems with cortisol and adrenaline. If these are in positive territory, we feel "safe". Leaders need to be aware of their impact on others and try to find ways to increase these factors at work in order to increase psychological safety. He calls this the SCARF model, which stands for:[5]

Status (and self-esteem): This refers to our feelings of importance or significance, relative to others. Status includes feelings of seniority, being respected, being admired/acknowledged, being consulted, receiving positive feedback/compliments, and having self-esteem. The 'threats' to status include being treated as someone of no importance, people talking down to you, humiliation, being ignored, being told what to do, and public criticism.

Certainty: This refers to a sense of familiarity, security and predictability and includes clear expectations, goals and plans, consistency, and clear rules and communication. The 'threats' to certainty include dealing with the unfamiliar, uncertainty and change, unclear expectations, goals and vague plans, inconsistencies, changing rules, half-truths or incomplete information.

Autonomy: This refers to having control or choice, i.e. being able to make your own decisions and managing your own time and workflow. The 'threats' to autonomy include micro-management, authoritarian management and inflexible rules.

Relatedness: This refers to being part of the group; being with people you know; having a sense of belonging, friendship and inclusion; and being with people you trust and who have similar values. The 'threats' include being ignored or excluded, distrust, being among people with different values, or being among strangers.

Fairness: This refers to a sense of justice and to rules that are applied consistently. The 'threats' include feelings of injustice and that there are different rules for different people.

This is an important model for leaders as it helps explain their own and others' reactions to events, e.g. why people engage or disengage, why people resist change, how changes in status affect people, why empowerment of people is important, why it is necessary to have good working relationships and good networks, and why people react so strongly to unfairness at work.

Figure 9: SCARF – A useful model for managing the team climate for high engagement

Back to Rochelle and Nicholas

At her second coaching session a month later, Rochelle reported that she had read up on psychological safety and reflected on the 12 action points she could work on. She had a meeting with her team where she spoke about what she believed in in terms of great teamwork. She took care not to sound as though she was criticising them and asked each person what kind of team they wanted to be part of. After some reluctance, people started to speak. The feeling was they were still getting to know her, which Rochelle interpreted as getting to trust her. It came out that the previous manager had a "my way or the highway" approach; he was very controlling and brutal if anyone made a mistake, so the team had become used to playing it safe and protecting themselves.

The team agreed on some norms in the form of "do more of", "do less of" and "keep on doing".

Meetings were starting to go better but there was still a long way to go in terms of each person's full engagement.

"To build confidence and energy in the team", said Nicholas, "my suggestion is that we start to explore each person's strengths".

Summary

Psychological safety is the foundation for a high trust, high engagement and high performance work climate. From a neuroscience perspective, creating a safe and trusting environment should be a top priority for leaders. Employees need to feel safe to speak up, ask questions, challenge ideas, own their mistakes and try out new ideas. Only then as leaders can we create an environment of highly engaged employees where real issues can be freely discussed and innovation can flourish.

An environment where people feel respected, heard, valued, supported and entrusted with meaningful work supports a sense of fulfilment and high engagement.

Reflection

In this chapter we identified 12 leadership practices to increase a sense of psychological safety in the workplace. Reflect on each one and make notes on what you believe you are doing well, as well as ideas for action

Principle	Doing well	Ideas for action
Trust		
Respect		
Collaboration		
Conflict		
Recognition		
Belonging		
Information sharing		
Change		
Learning from failure		
Allow people discretion		
Accessible		
Positivity		

Chapter 3

Aligning work to employees' strengths

In this chapter we focus on the importance of identifying employee's strengths and aligning their work to their natural talents.

"The purpose of life is to discover your gift; the work of life is to develop it; and the meaning of life is to give your gift away."

—David Viscott

"Stop trying to be more of who you're not and start focusing on what naturally makes you powerful and unique."

—Clifton Strengthsfinder

Nicholas explains the importance of knowing each person's strengths

Rochelle was intrigued by the idea of exploring strengths. "It's an important step in setting people up for success and high engagement", explained Nicholas.

Imagine going to work every day, knowing that for most of the day you will be doing what you love doing and do well. Your levels of engagement. success and happiness at work would be high.

This is the foundation of the strengths-based approach – find out what people do well naturally, align their work to that, and develop their skills in line with their natural talents.

Why focus on strengths?

As leaders, our role is to help bring out the best in people and support our team members' growth and development. The best leaders know that each person is different, that no one is good at everything, and that that's OK. They observe employees at their best in order to identify their natural talents as well as what they care about at work. They then put them into roles or on projects where these talents can develop into full-blown strengths.[49]

This is one of the most important aspects of employee engagement, as people who love their work have discovered what they are good at, i.e. their strengths, gifts brilliance, as well as what they care about: their passion. They have then found ways, usually with the support of their managers, to build these more fully into their roles at work.[50] They are connected to their "inner spark" and are experiencing high energy and liveliness at work.

When we tap into our gifts and talents, work flows with more ease and creativity. We also develop greater confidence and well-being as a result of the successes and enjoyment we experience. It is as though we are "firing on all cylinders". If we can achieve that, then work will not feel like work. Using our strengths well leads to success and happiness at work.

We all have natural talents – things we do almost instinctively. We then need to add knowledge, skills and experience until they become strengths.

When people talk about your strengths, they may say "you have a gift". And of course, gifts are something we give to others. We are meant to do something with our talents and if we don't, we feel unfulfilled.

Knowing our strengths is the first step

I am going to ask you to spend time or some important personal
reflections which will help you to identify your strengths. It is very
important that we have a good insight into our strengths as we will
make better career choices. I have known people who were very
successful in a particular job and because of their great reputation,
were offered other jobs. Before you accept a new position, think
about if it's a role that matches your strengths.

An example I came across as a coach was Joel, who was a top
performer in a big corporate and other areas in the company were
trying very hard to persuade him to move to one of their divisions.
Joel's strengths and the reasons for his success were his futuristic
and planning skills; he was able to see the direction his field was
taking and he was consistently ahead of the change curve. He
was working with a small team of specialists when an offer came
up for a big promotion, which he took. The new job was more of
a troubleshooting role requiring quick decisions and reactions to
problems, as well as managing a big team of semi-skilled people.
Within a year Joel had gone from a top performer to a poor
performer, with his confidence shattered and under huge stress.

Of course, this is not to say we must be over-cautious; we must take
on new challenges and there will be times when your intuition says,
"It's risky, but take it". Those changes may put you on a whole new
growth spurt and you may discover new strengths. Yet the more self-
aware you are regarding when you are at your best, the better choices
you will make about career moves as well as job roles and projects.

Martin Seligman, in his book *Flourish,* suggests that you should think
of your strengths as:

- how you stand out;
- your natural gifts/talents;
- what you love to do and do well;
- this feels like me;

- you feel happy and fulfilled when you are involved in these activities;
- other people tell you that you have a gift for this activity;
- you are attracted to this activity;
- you learn quickly how to do this;
- you look forward to engaging in this type of activity;
- you feel happy and confident when you do this;
- time stands still – you are totally engrossed;
- you are energised by it;
- it is internally motivated; and
- you can hardly stop yourself from using it whenever possible.[51]

Our strengths are a golden thread in our lives. It does not matter where we find ourselves, we will find ourselves expressing our strengths in one way or another. We feel as though something is missing when we cannot find an outlet for our strengths. The best scenario is when we use our strengths to make a difference to something important to us: then we are in our full power. When you are expressing your talents in the world you will be making your greatest contribution and feeling most successful and fulfilled. Your strengths or your gifts represent the "magic" within you and are key to your success and feelings of fulfilment.

You have strengths and your job is to identify them, develop them and put them to work.

People get a boost in energy and happiness when they use their strengths. When we are able to align our work to our strengths, we feel energised. We enter a state called "flow", which is when we are so absorbed that time passes quickly and what we are doing happens easily and naturally. Flow is "a state of being so intensely absorbed in and focused on an activity that a person loses their sense of time and their sense of self while their sense of control over their activity increases. Their actions flow effortlessly". The experience of flow leads to higher engagement levels, creativity and energy. This results in greater happiness and satisfaction. The conditions required for flow include a challenging situation, where someone can use their natural strengths and talents as well as activities, which are viewed by them as something of importance.[52]

When we are in flow at work, we tend to do our best work and experience an upward cycle of success leading to further success as our confidence and experience grows.[53]

Think about how this upward cycle might work:

- You work on a task that is in line with your natural talents and skills and that you feel passionate about.

- Because it is in line with your natural strengths, you look forward to this task.

- You learn what you need to know or are able to do it easily.

- You persevere if you come across obstacles because you want it to be a success because it is something you believe is important.

- You are successful at this task.

- Rewards follow: clients/customers and bosses are appreciative, you get recognition at work, and over time your skills and reputation grow and your career flourishes.

- Your self-confidence grows and you feel good about your work.

- As a result of your increased confidence, you take on bigger and more complex projects.

- You go through the same cycle, only at a higher level of complexity and skill.

This is the upward spiral, which is more likely to happen if you do work that is in line with your talents and passion.

This experience of "flow" at work, or the experience of being completely absorbed in an activity that one enjoys, is an important contributor to the quality of a person's work experience and engagement.[54]

Our strengths tend to be so embedded in who we are that we often don't even notice them; they become invisible to us. The reason for this is that there are things that we do so easily and so well, that it feels normal to us rather than something special. We think if it is easy for us, it will be easy for everyone. We know all about our weaknesses because if we have tried something and failed, that memory sticks with us. Our strengths are often more visible to other people who can see when we are at our best.

tips/ideas

In my coaching role, I often write to people who know the person I am coaching very well and I ask them to send me feedback on this person at their best. When the coachees read all the feedback, they are usually overwhelmed by it as they realise the positive impact they are having on the people around them. It is usually a complete blind spot for them.

It is important to acknowledge our own personal power; each one of us has special and unique gifts. They have most likely always been with us and they are what people most remember us by.

Our task as individuals regarding our natural talents is to identify them clearly, develop them into strengths and put them to work towards something we believe is worthwhile. We have to find the situations where our strengths can express themselves. When we are not in touch with our gifts or not using them, we always feel something is missing; there's a feeling of dissatisfaction and frustration. Our strengths are always looking for an outlet where they can express themselves.

We don't have only one talent or strength; we have a number of strengths and often it's the way they combine that gives us our uniqueness. Developing and using our strengths is part of the route to reaching our full potential, embracing our uniqueness and expressing ourselves fully. Because our strengths are unique, we need to find our own path where our strengths can be expressed fully.

> "How could you have a soccer team if all were goalkeepers? How would it be an orchestra if all were French horns?"
>
> **—Desmond Tutu**

Identifying your strengths

Now, how do you know what your real strengths and talents are? The clues are all around us; we have to observe ourselves and start to notice and appreciate things about ourselves that we usually take for granted.

Our strengths are an undercurrent beneath the surface of our lives. We need to observe how, in many seemingly different situations, we tend to engage in the same activity, as that is a clue to our strengths.

> "Everyone is a genius. But if you judge a fish by its ability to climb a tree, it will live its whole life believing that it is stupid."
>
> —credited to **Albert Einstein**

Questions to help you identify your strengths[55]

As a leader, start by doing this exercise first and see what themes start to emerge for you.

Then ask each team member to do the exercise for themselves and see what they come up with in terms of their strengths.

tips/ideas

Start by thinking back to good experiences. Think back to examples of things you feel you did well, enjoyed doing, gave you a sense of satisfaction and are proud of. List these achievements.

The achievements you list must be ones that made you feel particularly good, which you enjoyed doing and feel that you did well. Whatever you were doing just seemed to flow; things just came easily and naturally to you; there was little or no struggle. They can come from different periods of your life and from different aspects of your life. These achievements need to be things you have done, not just part of some great experience. Give concrete examples of what you were actually doing, for example, talking, listening, building, researching, creating etc.

Focus on what you **did**, not on what other people did or on the circumstances surrounding each event.

Then, from these experiences, look for common themes by creating two lists. The first list includes the verbs, i.e. the actions you took, while the second list includes the objects, i.e. what you took action on.

Verbs	Objects
I created...	A beautiful garden
I wrote...	A story for children
I developed...	A team dashboard to track KPIs

Once you have a nice long list of what you were doing in these situations, go back and circle the words in the lists above that feel like you at your best.

? What strengths were you drawing on to be successful? What was your contribution to a successful outcome? Look for the golden threads and common themes, e.g. I am creative, empathetic, entertaining, analytical etc.

---

tips/ideas

Remember, your strengths are always finding ways to express themselves. The activities that attract you are those that allow expression of your strengths. They are also likely to be the things you do best.

For further insights about your strengths, please also work through the following questions to help you further crystallise and confirm your thoughts about your strengths.

- What activities do you learn quickly and easily; what comes naturally to you?

- What activities make you feel happy and energised?

- Think of situations where you were in 'flow', i.e. it was easy to concentrate, you were absorbed and time just flew by? What are you doing when 'time stands still', i.e. you get completely engrossed and you lose track of time?

- What activities do you look forward to? What interests, engages and stimulates you the most? List them all. Your interests, skills and accomplishments are all expressions of your strengths. What is similar about these activities?

- What have others always said you are good at? In which situations do others look to you to take the lead because you know what needs to be done and how to do it?

- What do other people appreciate about you? When do people turn to you? When are you in demand?

■ What are the most consistent messages you have been hearing about your contribution/talents?

■ When working in a team, what is your special contribution to the success of the team? What do people get out of being with you? Is it your leadership? Your humour? Are you a natural organiser? A detail person? Are you the do-er? Do you see how to make an idea work?

■ What positive feedback have you received?

■ When at work do you feel most engaged? What energises you? When you are doing things that you enjoy and engage you, you are connected to your strengths.

■ Think of times when you experienced positive emotions at work because you were enjoying what you were doing, proud of the work you were doing, and enthusiastic about what you were doing.

■ What types of activities make you feel most happy and fulfilled when you do them over and over again? And what causes this happiness?

■ If you were given a free day at work to do whatever you like to do most, what would you choose to do? Or, when there is nothing to do or when you have a choice of what to do, what do you tend to do? Do you make things? Talk to people? Paint? Write? Tidy up? Ask why you do these things? What is it that you are trying to create or contribute? What makes it satisfying?

■ What drains your energy at work? And what is that the opposite of?

■ What feels "missing" from your work right now?

■ Whose job do you envy and why?

Finally, from all of this, identify what you love to do and do well. How do you stand out? What do you consider to be your greatest gifts? To do this, look at your answers to all the questions. See what goes together; look for common themes or the "golden threads" from all the examples listed above. For example, are your strengths working with people? Working with 'things'? Or in the field of ideas? Are they are a unique combination of those? Try to be specific. Look at possibilities below for some examples n each of those fields to further refine your thinking.[56]

People	Doing	Ideas, concepts or data
▦ Communicating ▦ Advising ▦ Teaching ▦ Listening ▦ Leading ▦ Entertaining ▦ Persuading ▦ Helping ▦ Coordinating	▦ Making ▦ Inventing ▦ Repairing ▦ Designing ▦ Growing ▦ Speed and agility	▦ Gathering information ▦ Researching ▦ Organising ▦ Analysing ▦ Synthesising ▦ Planning ▦ Tracking ▦ Writing ▦ Strategising

By studying your successes, you will uncove᠆ a pattern of talents. This pattern will indicate the kind of career activi᠆es that are likely to be a part of your future achievements, regardless what you are doing currently.

Now write a description of yourself that summarises and distils this information. This should weave together the themes from feedback you have received along with your self-observations into a composite of who you are at your best. Start with: "When I am at my best, I am contributing in the following ways..."

Confirm that these are your strengths by using the following checklist:

- ▓ I have been very successful at this type of activity.
- ▓ I would volunteer for this type of activity.
- ▓ I'm instinctively attracted to this type of activity.
- ▓ I like to perform this type of activity frequently.
- ▓ I learn very quickly how to perform this type of activity.
- ▓ I would like to learn new ways of doing this activity better.
- ▓ I feel happy when I do this type of activity.
- ▓ I go into "flow" when I am engaged in this activity.
- ▓ When I am working in alignment with these strengths, I feel energised and positive.

Confirming your strengths

You may find it interesting to do one of the well-known strengths tests to shed more light on your strengths.

CliftonStrengths (Gallup)[57]

One of the best known strengths tests is CliftonStrengths. You can complete it online for a report on your top five strengths, or for the complete list of your full 34 strengths ranked from highest to lowest. The best approach is to work with a certified Strengths Coach to get the full benefit from these reports, or you can work through it on your own, with a colleague or friend, or your manager.

- Review the top five strengths and the description of each one.

- Reflect on how each strength plays out in your life. Recall situations when you used those strengths and the impact they had, and how the use of each strength contributes to your team and job role, as well as to successes you have had.

- How do these compare to your own assessment of your strengths that you completed above?

The 34 Gallup strengths are clustered into four categories:

- Executing.
- Influencing.
- Relationship Building.
- Strategic Thinking.

People with strengths in the Executing domain know how to get things done; they take ideas and turn them into reality.

Those with strong Influencing strengths are persuasive and able to sell the team's ideas and achievements. When you need someone to speak up on behalf of the team, look to someone with the strength to influence.

Those strong in Relationship Building hold the team together and bring out the best in others.

People with great Strategic Thinking talents are focused on what could be. They absorb and analyse information that help us move forward and make better decisions. People with these strengths will continually stretch our thinking for the future.

The CliftonStrengths shed light on what you **DO** best, whereas the next strengths test, the VIA, is more about character strengths or who you are **BEING** at your best.

The VIA Character Strengths[58]

> @ You can take a free character strengths test at:
> http://www.viacharacter.org/character-strengths.

The VIA lists 24 character strengths which are divided into six clusters:

- Wisdom and Knowledge.

- Courage.

- Humanity.

- Justice.

- Temperance.

- Transcendence.

Your character strengths reveal your unique pathway to reaching your goals and have already played a significant role in your life. If you examine any of your top five strengths on the VIA you will come to the conclusion that they have been core to who you are and how you approach life.

Putting your strengths to work

The more we can align our job to our strengths, the more engaged and successful we are likely to be at work. So how are you using your strengths at work?

- To what extent is your work aligned to your strengths? How fully are your strengths being used at work?

- What tasks or roles are in line with your strengths and which ones are not?

- What possibilities do these strengths open up for you and what possibilities do they close down?

- What part of you wants to see the light of day at work? How can you spend more time in your 'talent zone', i.e. you do more of what you do best and less of what you don't do so easily and well?
  - Think of the activities in line with your strengths and what you love to do.
  - Think about how you actually spend your time and what do you do every day.
  - Compare the two lists.
  - What is the message?

- What situations do you regularly encounter where your strengths are not a good match?
  - Who in your team complements you in terms of strengths and should take responsibility for these situations? (Your strengths are not good for every situation, and in some situations, you can step back and let people with complementary skills step forward.)

- How can you make changes so you do more of what you do best and less of what you don't do easily and well?

- What could you introduce into your work that would shake things up positively?

- How can you use your strengths in a new way to address current workplace challenges or to create a new reality for yourself (adventure)?
  - If there is a block or conflict in your life at present, think about which talent or strength you have that you are currently not using to resolve the situation.

Job crafting: Aligning your work to your strengths

If you have compared your strengths with your daily work tasks and found some misalignments, you may consider some "job crafting". This refers to the steps people take to align their jobs more closely to their strengths and values. Job crafting has been shown to have an impact on an employee's sense of meaning and purpose at work, and therefore on their engagement.[59]

You may have to negotiate with your manager and your team to add or take away tasks so that your job is more fulfilling and a better fit with your personal strengths and values. Changes you propose making to your job must also create value for the team and the company, and be done for the right reasons and not just to get rid of the routine work that has to be done. Engaged people are more likely to job craft by seeking new challenges, e.g. by volunteering for projects.[60]

Job crafting helps employees to sustain their engagement. When employees craft their job in order to increase its meaningfulness, job satisfaction, engagement and performance all increase. Job crafting allows for employees to better utilise their strengths and pursue their passions and interests.[61]

To be engaged and happy at work, people need to learn how to create jobs that support their strengths, values and passions. This requires a high level of self-insight. People who find their work meaningful have taken personal responsibility and negotiated changes to their job to ensure it is significant to them.[62]

Managers need to be open to these kinds of discussions with employees and support job crafting if practically possible. When we align work more closely to people's strengths, everyone wins.

Reflective questions for job crafting

- In what way can you more fully use your strengths at work?
- How can you best develop your natural talents so you can become one of the best at performing this type of activity?
- What has been your best achievement this year? How could you use that experience to accelerate your success going forward?
- What might be some new ways you can use your talents to create high performance?

- In what ways can you best use your strengths and talents to make a difference at work?

What about weaknesses?

People are often very concerned about fixing their weaknesses and shortcomings; none of us can do everything well, but each of us can do something better than many other people. We each have unique talents and a unique way of expressing them, but there are also things we just don't do well.

Some weaknesses we can ignore as they are no obstacle to our success. Maybe I am not very artistic, but my role at work requires me to be pragmatic and find technical solutions, so who cares? Other weaknesses, however, may derail us, so we need to acquire some skills and knowledge to address those. We should not ignore weaknesses, but rather find ways to minimise their impact. It is rare that weaknesses will develop into strengths, but strengths can develop infinitely if we hone them through using them often and through development. This is how we bring out the best in people and raise engagement levels at work.

Take the scenario below. This person, Jeffrey, has a strength in Analytical activities but some weaknesses in the areas of Creativity and Interpersonal skills.

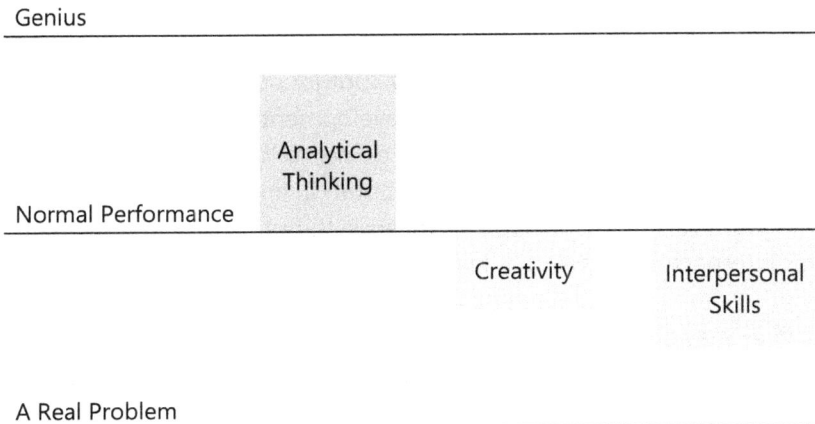

Genius
_____

Analytical
Thinking
Normal Performance
_____

Creativity   Interpersonal
Skills

A Real Problem
_____

Figure 10: An example of Strengths vs. Weaknesses

The first observation you might make when looking at Jeffrey's Analytical skills is that the distance to Genius level is not too far. With experience and development, Jeffrey can become highly skilled and the go-to person when you want to identify trends, investigate problems in-depth, develop business cases and so on.

Strengths that are over used can also become a weakness however, so Jeffrey needs guidance on when he should step forward and when he should hold back with his analytical skills. We have all used the term "analysis-paralysis" at times when someone will not make a decision because they want more and more information. And rational analysis can also inflame a situation when emotions are running high.

The second question is, should he go on a creative thinking course? Probably not; it will likely frustrate him and he will probably never be very creative. Rather use Jeffrey when analytical skills are needed.

However, does he need to acknowledge the contribution of creative people and be able to work in harmony with them? Absolutely. He needs to understand that in every project, there is a messy phase of divergent thinking which is not his comfort zone. So rather than rolling his eyes and critiquing half-formed ideas, he needs to allow the process to unfold. Once some ideas look promising, the team may turn to him for perspective and a detailed analysis on their feasibility.

In terms of interpersonal skills, Jeffrey is regarded as lacking in empathy and tact. This can derail his contribution in the organisation, so definitely some awareness and development is needed that at least brings him into the territory of doing no harm. It may never develop into a strength of his; his reputation and personal brand will no doubt rest on his strong analytical skills, but he should develop his interpersonal skills to at least an acceptable level.

Jeffrey may also decide to lean on one of his team members who is gifted with talents in bringing about harmony and consensus when he must face difficult conversations or conflict.

What part does the manager play in the strengths-based approach?

People want to do work they are good at and can feel good about; they want to play to their strengths. When employees are mismatched in a role, they will struggle to succeed and become bored and frustrated. They may not feel enthusiastic about being at work and they will have to look for enjoyment and a sense of purpose in weekend activities.

Managers must be able to talk to their employees about their strengths, helping them to identify and best leverage their talent, skills and knowledge. Managers also need to support employees to make changes to their jobs so their work is more closely aligned to their strengths.

A strengths-based approach is better for everyone as engagement levels and performance will soar.

When managers do not know and cannot leverage their employees' strengths, they diminish performance by preventing people from doing what they do best. Managers must thus help employees know their strengths and give them opportunities to consistently apply those strengths to their roles.

What part does each employee play?

One of the most important personal leadership skills is self-awareness; we must all discover what we are really great at. We need to identify those abilities that others admire in us and think about those activities that are so easy they just flow effortlessly. We must discover our talents and then work to develop them into strengths. If we focus on our strengths and improve our skills and knowledge daily, then over time we will become an expert at something and love our jobs. That is our responsibility if success and happiness at work is important to us.

Rochelle's experiences

Rochelle was very upbeat at her next coaching session with Nicholas. She proudly told him that she had read his notes on strengths, done the reflective exercises, asked her team to also complete them, and held a team session where each person shared their conclusions about their strengths. It turned out to be very affirming for people as team members confirmed each other's strengths and in many cases had added on a few more to each person's list.

The team spoke about job roles too. Rochelle mentioned that she had realised that the work of the team required a real mix of strengths. The team needed people to identify opportunities and problems; to share best practice information and make suggestions about the way forward; to evaluate those ideas; to plan and execute; to influence to get buy-in from others; to trouble shoot when the unexpected happened; and to coordinate to keep the team organised and focused.

Team members could immediately see where their strengths could be best used and some trading of tasks started to happen. People left the meeting very energised and excited.

"And what feedback did you get from the team?", asked Nicholas. "Fortunately they could see I have leadership and strategic skills", said Rochelle. "They also said I am good at delegating, but I think they were teasing me!"

"A suggestion from my side", said Nicholas, "is that you take this discussion further at your next round of performance review meetings and build on what you have started".

"I certainly will", said Rochelle, "so thanks, I think my problem has been solved".

"Not yet", said Nicholas, "there is more! People generally enjoy the process of discovering what they are good at, but employees' strengths also need a clear purpose. To be fully engaged at work, we need to be in situations where our strengths can express themselves. However it is not enough to be working on things we are good at; our work must also revolve around things we are passionate about and that give us a sense of meaning, purpose and contribution. That is our next topic for coaching".

Summary

People are at their best when their work makes use of their strengths. The best leaders identify each person's strengths and allocate work accordingly. This is a win-win approach; the employee loves his or her work and does it well, meaning the work of the team is of a better standard.

Application of these principles

Work through the reflective exercises in this chapter and ask your team to do the same.

Consider holding a team session where people can share their insights about their strengths and where their colleagues can add to their insights.

Make strengths and how to use them at work a topic in your annual performance review conversations.

"There is one thing in this world, which you must never forget to do.

Human beings come into this world to do particular work.

That work is their purpose, and each is specific to the person.

If you forget everything else and not this, there's nothing to worry about.

If you remember everything else and forget your true work,

then you will have done nothing in your life."

—Rumi

Chapter 4

Meaning, purpose and a sense of contribution at work

In this chapter, we explore the following topics:

- The importance of work with meaning and purpose in employee engagement.
- Clarifying an organisation or team's purpose through a vision and values statement.
- Bringing vision and values to life.
- Aligning company or team purpose to employees' values in order to provide a sense of meaning and contribution.

"Working hard for something we do not care about is called stress. Working hard for something we love is called passion."

—**Simon Sinek**, *Start with Why: How Great Leaders Inspire Everyone to Take Action*

"Few, if any, forces in human affairs are as powerful as shared vision. A shared vision is not an idea... it is rather a force in people's hearts... at its simplest level, a shared vision is the answer to the question 'What do we want to create?'"

—**Peter Senge**

"The best prize that life has to offer is the chance to work hard at work worth doing."

—**Teddy Roosevelt**

"Your real work is to figure out where your power base is and to work on that alignment of your personality, your gifts you have to give, with the real reason why you are here. Align your personality with your purpose, and no one can touch you."

—**Oprah Winfrey**

"Work is love made visible."

—**Khalil Gibran**

Rochelle and Nicholas discuss meaning and purpose at work

Nicholas arrived a little late and a bit flustered to the next coaching session. "So we're talking about meaning and purpose at work", he said. "A bit difficult to get excited about roof tiles but let's try!" "What do you mean?", said Rochelle. "Roof tiles are very important!" "Then help me out", said Nicholas, rolling his eyes. "What am I missing?"

"Your roof tiles are an important part of your building's aesthetics", said Rochelle. "The colour range and the styles all add to a building's appeal. And even more important, when there is hail, heavy rain, wind or baking sun, you want a roof tile that can withstand all of that and not crack, blow off, get brittle or fade. Otherwise you will have a shabby looking building and roof leaks damaging the interior of your house. Our roof tiles are top quality and fashionable; we make a great product range."

"I get it", said Nicholas, "roof tiles are important and you are proud of these products. So let's talk about how we can use this to build high engagement in your team".

Work with purpose and meaning

Imagine going to work each day to use your strengths in a way that makes an important difference to someone somewhere.

If you ever read articles about people who are successful, you will notice that the word 'passion' usually comes up in the article. Successful people are working at something they feel passionate about, whether its good coffee, natural beauty products, saving lives, beautiful furniture or buildings. Their passion for what they do gives them energy for the hard work needed to achieve their vision. Work involving activities and projects we are passionate about gives us the inner fuel to persevere and achieve great results.

Purpose, meaning, passion and the desire to make a positive difference to something important to us provides us with the energy to work at something for extended periods, overcome obstacles, be creative and innovative, and achieve lasting results. You work hard because you want to.

A sense of contribution, purpose or meaningful work is fast becoming a major contributor to engagement.[63] If my work allows me the opportunity to do something I am passionate about, and a feeling of making an impact and contribution in that I am making a difference to something important, my engagement at work increases significantly. I have a "career with heart"; a career that meets higher human needs such as loving the actual work itself and a feeling that I am making a significant difference to something important to me.[64]

Work is an important forum for giving people a sense of meaning, as people spend a large part of their lives at work and a sense of meaning and purpose increases engagement at work. I am engaged if my work is aligned with my values and I am passionate about what I do. Work can meet my needs for a feeling of personal significance, the opportunity to live out my values, a sense of personal fulfilment and achieving my potential.[65]

Money may attract me to a job, but work aligned to my strengths plus purpose, meaning and the prospect of doing something valuable will increase my level of engagement at work; I thrive and grow when I experience my job as meaningful. This in turn affects the performance and reputation of the company I work for. Work becomes a place to contribute.[66]

Employees, especially Millennials, expect more from leadership in companies

Purpose, meaning and contribution are particularly important to Millennials, i.e. those born between 1980 and 1996. They are fast becoming the largest group of employees and are starting to enter leadership roles themselves.

Organisations have to deal with rapid and complex changes driven by technological innovation, artificial intelligence, uncertain political and economic environments, new competitors, changing customer needs, changing employee demographics, as well as changing employee aspirations.[67]

As a result of all of this, noted Deloitte's *2019 Global Millennial Survey,* younger employees particularly expect more of their leaders and the organisations they work for.[68]

Younger workers believe that businesses should consider all stakeholders' interests, including employees, customers, suppliers, communities and the environment, as well as profits. Many Millennials are concerned about climate change and resource scarcity, and want their companies to reduce their impact on the environment as well as improve society.

However, their experience is that their employers tend to put profits above all else, which leaves them feeling like a commodity brought in simply to help make money for their employers.

Millennials want business leaders to make a positive impact on society and respond to their needs; they want to work for companies and leaders with a bigger vision and purpose than just making something and selling it at a profit. They increasingly want their organisations to be a force for good.

Millennials want to work for leaders who are visionary, ethical and agents of positive social change. They want leaders to commit to making a positive impact on the world, as well as prepare their organisations and employees for the changes that Industry 4.0 is causing. They further want to work for companies that are creating innovative products and services for their customers. Unfortunately, many Millennials see business leaders as having a negative impact on society.

Employees want to work for great managers and great companies with great reputations and cultures. They want to be able to trust the management of their company and the direction in which it is taking the company. Companies therefore need to show that they have a clear direction and purpose, and leaders must be able to make the link for employees as to how their work connects to that direction and purpose.

When employees do not view their job as important, a disconnect happens in the form of absenteeism, poor quality, employee turnover and less effort, all of which have an impact on company performance.

Employees want more than just a salary; they also want to feel their work is important. They want to work for organisations with an inspiring mission and purpose, and they want to see how their work connects to the purpose of the company. In a nutshell, they want to contribute.

It is important for employees to be clear about why the company exists and what it brings to the world. Work is an important part of life and people are more engaged if they do work that feels worthwhile, fulfilling and has meaning.[69]

Great employees want to work for great companies, and to be a great company we need talented and engaged employees. Business leaders must thus have a strategy and vision that benefits all of their stakeholders and creates a great employee experience. A company's purpose is important to employees; working for a company with a strong vision and purpose instils a sense of pride in employees and leads to higher levels of engagement.

Leaders must ensure that employees understand the organisation's vision and purpose and can see how their individual work supports this. If there is an alignment between the company's vision and values and the employees' values, then people feel "I belong here".[70]

Drudgery vs. purpose

An operator in the body shop of a motor manufacturing plant mentioned that her work was not important because all she did all day was weld some brackets which no-one would ever see onto the underbody of the car. Her supervisor explained that that bracket was an important part of the braking system of the car and took her to the section where the brakes were fitted. Her feelings about her job changed instantly when she saw the importance of her work.

A clerical worker completed a spreadsheet for her manager every month. She had no idea what the information was used for until one day she realised it made up an important part of the information pack used for sales forecasting. When she saw the purpose of this information, she could immediately see some improvements she could make to the way the information was presented.

Work with meaning and purpose is therefore a cornerstone of motivation. Work is an important place for giving people a sense of making a difference. We spend a large part of our lives at work and if we are able to live out our beliefs and values at work and experience a sense of fulfilment and a feeling of making an impact and contribution, we will love our work and be more engaged. People who feel that they are contributing to something important report higher levels of meaning in life and have higher scores on happiness, well-being, life satisfaction and work engagement.[71]

We need to look at meaning and purpose on two levels:

- Firstly, do I support the purpose, vision and values of the company? Do I believe in the products they make or the services they offer, as well as the way they go about their business? This is important to employees as I want to know, if I work hard, that I am supporting something I believe is important and valuable,

- Secondly, does my job give me a sense of meaning and purpose? Can I see how my work contributes to the vision of the company?

Organisational purpose

The most successful businesses have a clear sense of purpose
and leaders have an important role to play in helping employees
understand the importance of their work and how it supports this
purpose.[72]

When we talk about our purpose, either as companies, teams
or individuals, we are talking about our WHY: What inspires or
motivates us? What do we stand for? Our WHY is fuelled by our
personal values and beliefs. It can be hard to capture in words
because it is more of a feeling than a rational thought.[73]

The WHY is the purpose or cause that drives every one of us. When
we are living in alignment with our WHY, we feel most alive, positive
and energised. Companies and teams with a strong, consistent WHY
command trust and loyalty over time, so if we can put words to those
feelings, we will be able to inspire the right action from our people.

However, most organisations tend to only focus on WHAT they do and
HOW they do it – tactics and strategies – and they do not give much
thought about WHY they are important to anyone. Focusing only
on WHAT and HOW fails to inspire employees and customers. Work
without a sense of purpose or contribution can become drudgery.[74]

Does your organisation's purpose or vision inspire anyone?

Does your organisation have a vision, purpose or intention beyond
making a profit? Who benefits from your company's success and how
do they benefit? The most admired business leaders and companies
are energised by a powerful vision, for example Richard Branson,
Steve Jobs and Anita Roddick.

Virgin is known for challenging the status quo – taking on industry giants and championing people and the planet

Disruption is in Virgin's DNA and they have made sure this is captured in their purpose; the reason Virgin exists. Virgin Group's purpose is "changing business for good", which means thinking about the long term impact of the business decisions that they make today.

Having a clearly articulated, embedded and measurable purpose in every Virgin business that drives their decisions and fuels their success results in positive impacts on customers, people, communities and the environment.[75]

According to Branson, "the Virgin values have and will always be the same: to change the game and challenge the status quo by providing a product or service of great use. My first business venture was Student magazine. Along the way, we saw gaps in the market where Virgin could play a role and can be an incredible force for good, and that's become our motto. If you love what you do and if you believe in what you do, others will share your enthusiasm. Passionate people find their way to the Virgin Group, and when they do, we snap them up and try to keep them within the family.

"Many of our products and services come about because we pay attention to what the market is missing or what's not being done well. The commitment is about doing things differently.

"Our strategy has been to screw business as usual. To look at what it is our customer wants, and what it is the industry needs, and to go in and exceed their expectations. And we've been successful not by wasting time scrutinising our competitors but by looking at ourselves from the point of view of our customers do and seeking feedback through listening."[76]

An interview with Steve Jobs, CEO of Apple

"What is your vision for the personal computer?" Campbell asked Jobs. Campbell said what happened next still gives him goose bumps. "Steve Jobs was a magical storyteller," Campbell told me. "For the next hour, he talked about how personal computers were going to change the world. He painted a picture of how it would change everything about the way we worked, educated our children and entertained ourselves. You couldn't help but buy in." Vision, said Campbell, was the one thing that separated Steve Jobs from the others.[77]

Oprah Winfrey, founder of OWN (the Oprah Winfrey Network) describes her purpose

"To be a teacher. And to be known for inspiring my students to be more than they thought they could be."[78]

The Body Shop, founded by Anita Roddick

"Never afraid to stand out from the crowd and stand up for what's right, we search the world for the finest ethically-sourced ingredients to create a range of naturally-inspired beauty products.

"Today our dedication to business as a force for good is stronger than ever. As part of our Enrich Not Exploit™ Commitment, we've made it our mission to enrich our products, our people and our planet. That means working fairly with our farmers and suppliers and helping communities thrive through our Community Trade programme, being 100% vegetarian and always and forever being firmly against animal testing.

"The business of business should not be about money. It should be about responsibility. It should be about public good, not private greed."

—Anita Roddick[79]

As leaders in business, we need to reflect on our values and ask ourselves what kind of business we want to run or what kind of team we want to lead, and how we can be a force for good while making a profit.

Having an inspiring purpose makes work more rewarding than just making a profit. The work begins to matter more to everyone. Working towards a higher purpose generates positive energy in leaders and employees as work becomes more satisfying and enjoyable. The alignment between personal and organisational values and goals supports high engagement.[80]

A purpose or vision should create the spark and the excitement that lifts an organisation out of the ordinary. A vision should energise people and encourage them to work together. The vision should provide the over-arching goal, i.e. the "why". This provides the 'compass' to keep the organisation focused and on track. A vision also encourages a long-term perspective.

A vision answers the question, "What do we want to create?" If we are able to create a shared vision, we will also create a sense of community and encourage collaboration across the company. When people share a vision, they are connected and bound together by common aspiration.

If being a contribution produces so many benefits, why don't all leaders work at clarifying an inspiring vision? The reason is that not all leaders believe in a purpose for business beyond making a profit. Only "transformational leaders" (see Chapter 6 on the Barrett model) are likely to create organisations of higher purpose.

The starting point for creating a sense of purpose is the creation of a clear statement, capturing and conveying what is most important about the organisation: its vision, purpose and values and how it intends to relate to customers, employees and other stakeholders. Vision and purpose statements have more impact if they are simple, idealistic, timeless, challenging and realistic. They should provide a sense of direction that is related to the bigger purpose of the organisation and encourage creativity and initiative.

How to define our WHY: purpose, vision and contribution

"Leadership requires two things: a vision of the world that does not yet exist and the ability to communicate it."

—Simon Sinek

Some company vision statements are described in very broad and general terms. This allows for flexibility, but the problem is that when we communicate our vision or purpose in this way, different employees have a different understanding of what we mean. The more concrete a vision statement is, the more effectively it can inspire employees.

An inspiring vision describes a clear picture of success, such as when Bill Gates imagined a "computer on every desk and in every home". Clarifying our WHY, whether at the company, team or personal level, can help us to formulate a vision and values that inspire people, as well as provide guidance on how to act in line with that.

At its core, a company's vision, purpose or mission is a statement of its reason for being in business and the contribution it intends to make. A team WHY is the contribution the team makes to the company's purpose and vision. And to feel inspired as an individual, we need to clarify our personal WHY; what are we passionate about and what are our personal values? What is our definition of a life well-lived?

People want to be part of something big. They want to work for leaders who give meaning to their work.

Definitions of terms

Purpose (or mission): A concise statement of why the organisation exists and what it does.

Core values: Qualities essential to the organisation's success – like financial sustainability or reliability.

Vision: A clear statement of a future result or end state that the organisation wants to achieve.

Goals: The priorities for realising the vision, purpose and values.

Objectives: Measurable results toward achieving the goals.

Action plans: Actions to be taken in support of objectives, with timelines and responsible people identified.

Developing a company and team vision, purpose and values

Developing a vision or purpose statement s not a mechanical process, but requires a deep understanding of the company, its products, its culture and its people.

A vision is sometimes created by the leader of a company or by the leadership team. A shared vision is created when leaders follow a wide consultative process and align their vision with the vision and values of employees and other stakeholders. A shared vision is something that people are truly committed to, because it reflects their own personal vision; it lifts their aspirations. People become excited about a vision they truly want to accomplish.

The vision going forward may emerge from a combination of past achievements, current capabilities and future possibilities. It is important to dialogue about these topics with a wide range of people, as well as to reflect on what you are personally passionate about as a leader until a strong theme emerges.[81]

- With key members of the company or team, reflect on your company or team's past. Recall good stories of when and how this company or team had a positive impact and made a difference.

  - List all the things that make you proud of the company or team.

  - Identify insights and recurring themes about the company or your team at its best. What was the impact on others?

- Engage with a wide range of stakeholders and listen to their views and stories about your company at its best, the impact of your products or services on them, and how they experience doing business with your organisation.

  - Again, capture insights and themes.

Then imagine the company or team in the future:

- Talk to stakeholders, i.e. customers, suppliers, employees and shareholders, about the company or team in the future. Explore what they need from your company or team and its products and services going forward.

  - What would delight them?

☐   What do they want from you going forward?

☐   What would you like them to say about you in the future?

Crystallise your thoughts by doing some "time travel" into the future. Imagine it is five years into the future. What do you want to see? What will make you proud?

■   In your mind's eye, imagine you are looking at the achievements of your company or team over the next five years. See yourself walking through your company or team location; you are on your way to an awards ceremony. The company has been immensely successful: customers, consumers, employees and shareholders have voted it "Best Company in its Class". Or, your team has been awarded "The Most Amazing Team" award.

■   What has happened to make them say this?

■   What value have you added to people s lives? Think about the customer first; what has your company/team done to make them feel so positive? What have you meant to them and their business and their lives? And now, the employees who love working there; why is that the case? What is it like working for the company/team? And then, your other stakeholders; they are smiling; what have you done for them? How have we made the world a better place?

As you go through this process, let images come to mind and write key word and phrases on cards that capture what you wish to create in your company or team for customers, employees and stakeholders. Then let it 'brew' for a few days until the right words emerge. Finally, bring all your thoughts together. As a business leader, what do you believe in? What kind of business do you want to create? What kind of team do you wish to lead? What are you passionate about?

The words you are looking for are those that describe:

- your contribution to the lives of others;

- the impact of your contribution; and

- the values that will drive behaviour in your company or team.

You might be thinking, but we make paper serviettes or we sell dishwashing liquid. How can that inspire anyone? So think beyond WHAT you do and think of what kind of business you want to run and the reputation you wish to have. For example:

- Your product might make a huge difference to the quality of life for some customer group. The impact of your product or service could be convenience, better health, a better quality of life, feeling safer, protecting wealth, more beautiful surroundings etc.

- Maybe you want to be known as a trusted supplier of high quality, reliable components that contribute to the quality and reliability of the product your customer manufactures.

- Customer experience may form part of your vision: what will it be like doing business with your company and team?

- Maybe your company is an innovator in production processes and systems which allows for higher volumes, better quality, reliable delivery, more flexibility and quicker turnaround times.

- It could be that your service offering is unique in some way.

- Perhaps your company or team has deep expertise in a particular field; maybe you have the greatest technical staff who understand your customers' needs and are able to design top quality products to match these.

- Maybe you are the "greenest" manufacturer in the industry, or you offer the most environmentally friendly products. Maybe your company is leading the way in terms of the environment by working to reduce the impact of your product or service on the environment and replenishing the environment where possible through recycling programmes, "green" workplaces, using renewable energy sources in the workplace, purchasing materials from organic or sustainable farmers, or adopting sustainable product packaging, for example.

▨ Part of your vision might also include what it will be like to work here. What can employees expect of the company or team in terms of employee experience? Will employees experience an innovative environment, growth and development, work-life balance, or a strong team culture? Your focus might be on your people through the creation of positive workplace cultures, employee development or improved employee benefit programmes.

▨ You may have a vision for making a difference to the community through programmes such as:

  □ local community outreach programmes;

  □ donating time, money or products towards various non-profit organisations;

  □ creating a foundation which works with one particular cause, e.g. becoming involved with social or political campaigns to protect the environment, animals or people; or

  □ providing assistance to communities that supply your raw materials or that manufacture materials for you.

Identifying your company's values

For people to feel engaged, they need to fit in with the culture of their company, i.e. they need to agree with "the way things are done around here".

Leaders need to manage the culture of their company. To do this they need to reflect on the values and behaviours required to support their vision. Values guide behaviour in a company or team and over time, the behaviours create a culture. Values set the tone in the workplace for how the work is to be done; they set the direction and give employees guidelines on how they should act and how they should approach situations at work.

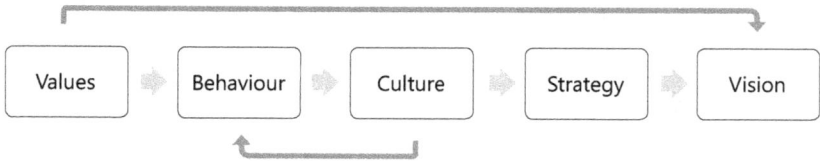

Figure 11: How values support company vision and strategy

As leaders, we need to ensure that our company values are the right ones to support the achievement of our organisation's vision. If you reflect on the vision and purpose of your company or team, ask yourself what values you believe are essential to support that vision and purpose, which make it a great place to work.

Once the values have been identified, the specific behaviours that support each value also need to be clarified.

Some examples of values and behaviours might be:

- **Innovation:** Be curious, experiment with new concepts, immerse yourself in new experiences.

- **Integrity:** Be honest and trustworthy, be ethical and do the right thing at all times, keep commitments, apply company policies fairly and consistently.

- **Collaboration:** Work cooperatively with other teams and departments, offer support to other teams so that corporate goals can be achieved, communicate and share information with others, give recognition and share the credit for progress and achievements.

It is important to define the values and behaviours you expect from employees as these create the workplace culture, or "how we do things around here". The reason we define values is to shape the behaviours of employees to create the desired culture, as the company's culture plays a big role in its ability to achieve its purpose and vision.

We want a company culture built on shared values that supports the vision, but we may find that our existing culture gets in the way of this. For example, if our vision requires innovations in our product range and the current culture is one where you don't rock the boat, it will be very difficult to make our vision a reality.

Unless you are starting a new company, the workplace already has a culture, which may or may not be relevant for the vision going forward. The values that prevail are the values that are most often reinforced and rewarded. As leaders we need to start by identifying the culture that already exists by asking ourselves how we typically do things here. Then we need to ask ourselves if that is the best culture to drive our organisation's or team's success going forward. Most companies operate on a default culture and we simply continue with the existing way of doing things.

The values that exist are either a reflection of the current leaders' underlying beliefs, or they are the heritage of past leaders. If you look at the behaviour of leaders, you can tell what the values of a company really are.[82]

Vision and values implementation

We may have a great vision as leaders, but how do we win the support and full engagement of our team to help bring our vision to life?

Conscious action, beginning with vision, purpose and values, is the starting point for creating a culture that will make a company great, and a great vision and culture create high engagement.

Formulating a clear and inspiring vision is only the first step in creating a company with a higher purpose, yet many business leaders think their work is done once they have done that.

Implementing the vision is the leader's next challenge

Talented employees who join your company because your vision and values resonate with them will be quickly disillusioned if they realise it's a paper exercise with nice posters on the wall and an appearance in the business plan and annual reports, but is never applied in creating the organisation's culture.

To bring a vision and values to life, leaders need to:

- communicate the vision, values and expected behaviours, and check people's understanding of these. This could be done in vision and values workshops where employees gain an understanding of what this means for them at work. One company used industrial theatre to communicate their values in an impactful and humorous way. As far as possible there should be dialogue with employees about the vision and values to achieve buy-in and understanding;

- talk about vision and values on an ongoing basis, encouraging employees to ask questions and providing them with examples of what living the vision and values looks like;

- use the vision and values to evaluate decisions: will this course of action support our vision and purpose? When the vision and values messages are clearly understood, employees know which actions are acceptable and which are not. Success is doing the right things the right way; and

- act in line with the organisation's vision and values at all times. They must be role models and ensure that their actions and words support the vision and values. Everything leaders do and say can either strengthen or destroy their efforts to change their culture. Damage is done by actions and words that are contrary to the values we say are important. For example, if a leader says that customer delight is the vision and then does not follow through on a promise made to a customer, the message and actions are inconsistent. The same happens if we say that respect is a core value but we resolve conflicts aggressively, or excellent quality is a value and we let substandard work go through.

Employees are very quick to pick up on a leader's mixed messages.

The actions the leader takes and the words they use give employees messages about what is really valued. When these messages are consistent, employees know where they stand. The best leaders understand the impact their actions have on how employees behave every day. Leaders must be congruent; their words and actions must support one another.

How leaders behave towards one another also reflects their real values. Leaders who focus on power and internal competition create toxic environments. A leadership team should thus work together to bring the vision and values to life and create a strong culture.[83]

Any organisational transformation begins with the transformation of the leaders. Organisations transform when leaders transform! Leaders who are good role models build the loyalty and commitment of their employees.[84]

- Leaders need to create a culture of openness and trust where people can challenge behaviours and practices that are not in line with the organisation's values. Leaders must also be courageous enough to address those who don't live the vision and values, otherwise their ideal culture will not happen.

  - One top management team introduced a Values Reflection at the end of their meetings, where they reflect on their own behaviour in the meeting and give feedback to each other. In this way the values are kept top of mind and consistently reinforced.

- Find ways to recognise and reward the behaviours you do want. Acknowledge employees when you see them acting in line with the organisation's vision and living the values. Show appreciation for change, initiative and innovation.

- Recruitment and performance appraisal methods must be revised to select and recognise people who display the values that are important to your company.

- [ ] If the vision requires new skills, recruit and empower innovative people to help make it a reality.

- [ ] Recruitment processes need to identify people who believe what your company believes and want to help you make the vision a reality.

- [ ] Some companies measure and reward people who live the values through a 360-degree assessment.

- [ ] Many companies include their values and expected behaviours in their performance review documents.

- Encourage and reward learning that supports the vision. Ensure you also value, respect and preserve past learning.

- Update and develop the organisation's processes and systems if needed for the vision to become a reality.

- To achieve the "why", leaders should encourage new ways of thinking and acting. Test proposed innovations that support the vision with small-scale experiments.

- To experience a sense of purpose and meaning at work, employees need to know how their company or their own work impacted a customer and how it improved their business or life. Employees who have direct contact with the beneficiaries of their work display greater persistence and experience greater meaning in their work.[85] Many people do work that affects the well-being of others, but often they never have the chance to see or meet the people affected by their work. Few leaders take the initiative to show how employees' day-to-day work benefits others. It is possible to create work environments where employees understand the impact of their work and this usually leads to greater engagement levels. Ways to do this could include:

  - [ ] encouraging employees to visit the end users of your product. A lack of contact with customers often means a poor understanding of the impact of your work. By making it a priority to spend time with your customers, you can gather information about their needs and your contributions. A connection to real-world customers and seeing first-hand how their work is beneficial to other people helps employees to see how their actions add value for customers, and from this they may develop a stronger sense that their work makes a difference. This makes people feel more valued and appreciated, which in turn increases engagement. As a leader, you are a link between your employees and your end users, so use your network to find clients and customers of your company's products and services who have great stories to share;

☐ asking employees to reflect on their successes and contributions as a way to reinforce the sense that their jobs matter. This reflection energises people;

☐ encouraging employees to be a client or customer as a way to experience how their work makes a difference. Using your organisation's products or services can shed new light on the consequences of your job. For example, at Patagonia, founder Yvon Chouinard encourages leaders and employees to field-test outdoor sports products. At VWSA, employees are given the opportunity to drive and experience the cars they build. In addition, the industrial engineers work on the production line as a way to experience the life of a production operator and to identify ways to improve ergonomics and productivity. The more experience people have with their organisation's offerings, the more they can understand the end user's perspective and understand the impact of their work;

☐ inviting end users to visit the organisation to interact with employees and explain their experience of the company's product or service. This will give employees an enriched understanding of the purpose behind their jobs; and

☐ explaining to employees how their work contributes to the vision of the company. For example, employees who train production operators need to track quality problems on the line and help staff to gain the necessary skills to improve quality. Watching these quality problems reduce will be a big motivator for the training person. A purchasing person needs to see the impact of their activities on both the quality and cost of the company's final product, while the marketing person needs to see the impact of their campaigns on sales.

- ■ Use the company's vision and values to inspire employees to be their personal best.

  - □ Remind people that living the values not only makes the company great, but it lifts each employee's contribution and reputation to new heights and each person becomes a better version of themselves.

  - □ Stretch people's thinking by challenging their existing assumptions and opening their minds to new possibilities.

  - □ Think about placing a visual reminder in the workplace that reconnects the work of the team to their larger purpose. Maybe it's a thank you note from a client, a photo of the people who benefit from your work, or an article highlighting the work your organisation does. Refresh these regularly as a way of getting people to think about WHY they do what they do.

Engagement increases when company and personal values align

As a leader, it is very important to find people whose values are in line with the company's vision and values. In *Good to Great,* Jim Collins said that it is important to get the right people on the bus (values) and in the right seats (strengths and skills).[86]

The alignment of my values to my work and to the vision and values of the organisation is an important driver of engagement.[87] This is a significant contributor to engagement, commitment and satisfaction, and to reducing anxiety and work stress.[88] Values are at the core of who people are and play a significant role in whether people feel they belong in an organisation. If there is alignment between the person's values and the organisation's values, or the way things are done at work, people feel a sense of belonging.

Managers who are clear about their organisation's values and who believe that their personal values are closely aligned with them have the most positive feelings about their organisations. They also express more commitment to their organisation and enjoy feelings of personal success and engagement, as well as lower stress and anxiety levels.[89]

Important conversations managers need to have with their people are around how they support the company's vision. This is the part we often forget. Each employee needs to be reminded that what they do is important. Every production operator has an impact on the quality of the final product and the reputation of the company; every person who talks to a customer has an impact on their view of the company and whether they want to continue doing business with it. The people that HR recruit and train has a big impact on whether the company is able to achieve its vision, as well as the people who buy the parts, get them to the line, and sell the products. We need to remind people that how they go about their work has an impact on the company's vision and values, i.e. their work is an important contribution to the bigger picture.

In real life... Patagonia makes clothes for outdoor sports

If you look at their mission and values as a prospective employee, you will know immediately if you want to be part of what they stand for and if you will fit in with their culture.

Our Mission: We're in business to save our home planet

Values

- Build the best product
- Cause no unnecessary harm
- Use business to protect nature
- Not bound by convention

Recruitment: If you care about having a company where employees treat work as play and regard themselves as ultimate customers for the products they produce, then you have to be careful whom you hire, treat them right, and train them to treat other people right. Otherwise you may come to work one day and find it isn't a place you want to be anymore.

We don't want someone who can just do a job; we want the best person for the job. Yet we don't look for "stars" seeking special treatment and perks. Our best efforts are collaborative, and the Patagonia culture rewards the ensemble player while it barely tolerates those who need the limelight.

We also seek core Patagonia product users, people who love to spend as much time as possible in the mountains or the wild. We are, after all, an outdoor company. We would not staff our trade show booth with a bunch of out-of-shape guys wearing white shirts, ties, and suspenders any more than a doctor would let his receptionist smoke in the office. We can hardly continue to make the best outdoor clothing if we become primarily an "indoor" culture. So we seek out "dirtbags" who feel more at home in a base camp or on the river than they do in the office. All the better if they have excellent qualifications for whatever job we hire them for, but we'll often take a risk on an itinerant rock climber that we wouldn't on a run-of-the-mill MBA. Finding a dyed-in-the-wool businessperson to take up climbing or river running is a lot more difficult than teaching a person with a ready passion for the outdoors how to do a job.

Of course we do hire some people strictly for their technical expertise. We have employees who never sleep outside or who have never peed in the woods. What they all do share, as our organizational development consultant noted, is a passion for something outside themselves, whether for surfing or opera, climbing or gardening, skiing or community activism.

(Excerpt from *Let My People Go Surfing*, by Patagonia founder/owner Yvon Chouinard)[90]

My individual purpose

"Don't ask what the world needs. Ask what makes you come alive, and go do it. Because what the world needs is people who have come alive."

—Howard Thurman

As leaders we need to gain an understanding of our own values and passions, as well as understand what is important to the people we lead.

Values, passion or what gives us a sense of meaning and purpose is a bit like an underground stream that we need to tap into on a regular basis. We can sometimes lose touch with this and life goes onto auto pilot; we are busy but maybe not fulfilled. Increasingly people are feeling that their work is not just a job but an important part of their lives. They spend a lot of time working, so that time must contribute to their overall well-being. A sense of purpose, fulfilment and contribution is an important part of well-being.

> David was a lawyer and he was not feeling very energised; the pressure was high and there were too many issues to deal with. As his coach, I asked him what his intention was as a lawyer. As he spoke, he became alive again: his choice as a lawyer in every case was to either go for a win at all costs, or to be a fair lawyer and find solutions that are just to both parties. He realised that he felt most alive when he achieved a fair outcome for both parties and that was the reputation he wanted. With a clear intention, his energy levels and passion for his work returned.
>
> Jess was working on a project to make a business case for a new product. She was putting in very long hours and re-working the figures over and over again to strengthen her case. I asked her what energised her about this project and she spoke at length about the new jobs this would create in the long term and the boost to the local economy. Just talking about the potential impact of her work brought her fresh energy and determination.

When it comes to work, we need to reflect often on the below:

- What would i like to be part of or contribute to?
- How would i like to make a difference at work?
- Is there something i feel "called" to do?
- What would i love to create?
- What gets me interested and "fired up"? What "lights" me up?

- What am i most curious about and want to be more involved in?

- Is there a "burning question" i want to answer?

- What would i like to be an expert in?

- What would create a sense of meaning and purpose for me at work?

- What gives me a sense of fulfilment and satisfaction at work?

- What inspires me?

- What are my personal values and principles?

- What is my definition of a meaningful work life?

- If you think about your strengths and passions, how can work allow you to express these more fully? How can you use your brilliance to support your passion and make a positive difference at work?

- What is your voice of "no" saying?

- What is your voice of "yes" saying? What part of you wants to see the light of day at work? What changes for you at work are waiting to happen?

- What would the future you like the present you to do now and in the near future to make sure this part of your career contributes to that vision?

Does your job feel purposeful?

Make a list of what you are passionate about, what inspires you, what you want to do more of, and how you want to make a difference at work.

Then make another list of your current tasks, projects and activities at work.

Looking at the list of your current activities, tick off the ones that are currently in line with your personal passions and strengths.

Then create a new list of projects or tasks that are in line with your strengths and passions that you would love to be part of your role at work. Think about how you can start to bring those into your role at work. Who do you need to talk to and whose permission do you need? This is probably a good discussion to keep for your performance appraisal when your manager asks you about career aspirations.

This is important ongoing reflection as it's hard to be fully engaged doing work you do not feel passionate about or that is not in line with your strengths. Your energy at work soon gets drained and you are unlikely to be very successful. You need successes at work to draw new opportunities your way, so we all need to gradually move towards work we love. When we love what we do, we will experience greater success. In turn, this will build confidence and pride and open new doors for us at work.

Rochelle shares her experiences with Nicholas

"This was certainly thought-provoking", said Rochelle. "I had a discussion with my team about this."

"I hope you found they had a passion for roof tiles", said Nicholas, trying to look innocent.

"Actually they do", said Rochelle. "I first asked them how they felt about the company vision and values and if they felt connected to them. Fortunately my team loves the company's products and feels proud of them. Our roof tiles are really stylish and have been used by architects in some new, expensive and high profile developments. It makes the team proud. They also relate to the values and believe they are "right". Of course, we all see examples of where they are not being lived in the company, but overall they feel they fit with the culture.

"Then we discussed our team's purpose; there was a lot of debate around how we market our company's products and the ethics of marketing, but overall the team felt we play an important role in explaining to the market what our products are about and we believe our own marketing messages. The ethics of customer analytics was quite a discussion with team members questioning how far we take it. We did not finalise a purpose or vision statement for the team, but there were a lot of ideas about the significance of our role. The team felt that architects, builders and developers need to know about the great quality products we make and how our products beautify buildings. There was also a feeling that we need to spend more time researching building trends and work more closely with the product development team so that together we make sure our products remain appealing. Ideas started flowing in terms of how we could go about this.

"We decided to put up a poster of a beautiful new building using our roof tiles as a way to remind us that our purpose is get more of our product out there so that we have more stylish buildings in the country.

"Then in terms of personal passion and purpose, it was a good follow on from the strengths conversation as I asked each person what part of this was "calling" them. People spoke about how they would like to contribute and what would energise them at work. We spoke about longer term career issues and how current roles could evolve in line with strengths and passion. I have a person who loves promotions and events and really wants to develop in that field. I have a person who loves working on the web site and wants further development and involvement there. Another person loves the retail business and has ideas on new types of sales outlets. So I need to pick up on all of these ideas and make some shifts in who does what without upsetting anyone.

"It was such a great conversation", said Rochelle. "We've really turned this team around."

"Well done", said Nicholas. "The team sounds really inspired. So, does everyone know what their exact role is going forward and how the team will proceed with these great ideas? The details of who does what are clear to everyone?"

Rochelle's eyes widened. "Not yet", she said.

"That's your next step", explained Nicholas. "Otherwise you had a fun afternoon talking about what could be out it's business as usual. That will really disillusion your team. Clarity s very important for people. People want to know what their role is, what everyone else's role is, what their key tasks are, and what the deliverables are, i.e. what success will look like.

"When people have clearly defined and achievable goals that are shared freely, everyone feels more comfortable and more work gets done. Goals need to be aligned in the team and they have to be revisited and discussed regularly. We mustn't write down annual goals and then look at them at the end of the year. We need to discuss our goals and our progress at least quarterly.

"It helps engagement when people know what to do, when they see what others are working on, and the measurement of their performance is clear. And most importantly for the engagement of the team, as people achieve their goals and KPIs, they experience a sense of achievement and success, which builds confidence and well-being at work."

"I'm not sure I know where to begin", said Rochelle, starting to feel a knot in her stomach.

Clarity of roles and results

> "My boss bites off more than I can chew."
>
> **—Disgruntled employee**

"My suggestion", said Nicolas, "is to start a spreadsheet where you list the major roles, such as Sales Forecasting, Sales Outlets, Advertising, Special Promotions etc, and the key activities that go with each role.

"Then the innovations the team was talking about, you can add as part of an existing role or you can list them as new stand-alone projects.

"Once you have that list, it's a case of allocating a name next to each role. Try to keep all the tasks that go with a role together, but if it's a very big role, you may consider splitting it, as long as its practical to do so.

"Stand-alone projects can be allocated to one person or to a small team, but be clear on who the project leader is.

"The next step is to ask each person to write up their roles and responsibilities. Your company most likely has a performance management form, but if not, devise your own." Nicholas quickly sketched an example:

Name:	Job Title:	Period:
Role and Objectives	Measurable Outcomes (Key Performance Indicator)	Progress
Special Promotions To organise a promotion for architects, builders and developers in the Gauteng region so that they are aware of our full product range and the quality of our products	■ Attended by min 250 people ■ Budget : R400 000 ■ Timing: 1st quarter ■ Event to be rated as Excellent by 80% of attendees	

"As you can see", said Nicholas, "you're agreeing on what success will look like, not telling people how to do their job. You've also linked work to purpose. The person now knows what is expected and can use their own discretion on how to proceed. Of course, you're not abdicating: you'll ask the person to share their ideas with the team and get further input, and you'll hold progress reviews where you can guide and coach as required. The less experienced the person, the closer you'll stay to the project and probably the more input you'll give.

"By agreeing roles, specific objectives and performance measures, you're closing the loop on the Strengths conversation and the Purpose conversation; you're taking all the great ideas and bringing them to life. This will have a big impact on your team's engagement as they can see you are walking the talk not just talking the talk!"

"Ok", said Rochelle, "I've got this...".

"Not so fast", warned Nicholas. "One more step is required! Once people have defined their roles at work, you need to consider the Job Demands vs. the Resources they have to do the job."[91]

"For job demands, look at the volume of work and the complexity of the work. Then consider the resources available to the employee to do the job: think about the employee's skill level, confidence, resilience, support, time for the task, systems and processes, budget etc.

"If there is an imbalance and the demands are greater than the resources, the result is disengagement. The person will probably give up if they think there is no chance of success.

"And consider the remuneration aspect too. If the employee is taking on a much higher level of work, he or she may have expectations of a pay rise. Now we know money is not a factor in engagement, but if there is a perceived unfairness, it will lead to dissatisfaction which will affect the person's engagement. Exercise good judgement before finalising each person's job role!"

Summary

A compelling vision energises and engages people and encourages creativity and collaboration, as people want to be connected to something important and meaningful to them.

A clear organisational vision and values are key to success. It will help potential employees to decide if they want to be part of your vision and it will help you as the leader to identify who can best help you achieve the vision.

Leaders need to be totally committed to the vision and purpose of their organisations; employees want to know you are serious, as a values-rich culture needs leaders who live their companies' values and inspire top performance in others. Leaders need to create a culture where the vision can flourish.

Clear purpose and values empower people as they gain an increased sense of autonomy, competence, impact and meaning. When people understand what is required and why, they are more likely to want to contribute more and may go beyond their narrow job description to innovate, learn and support each other. This creates an upward spiral; the more successful we feel, the more engaged we become and the more we want to do, which leads to more successes.

As leaders we need to ask ourselves:

▪ Is our vision and values inspiring to our employees and customers?

- Do our stated values represent what we are today?

- Are the meanings of the values clear?

- Do we as leaders live the vision and values and if not, what do we do about that?

- Do our vision and values drive the decisions made in our organisation?

- Are our values integrated into the recruitment, performance review and reward processes?

- What do we do about people who do not live the values?

- Are we recruiting and promoting people who believe what we believe and have the energy and persistence to bring our vision to life?

The conclusion is that clarity around organisational vision and values, as well as alignment to employees' values, are important factors in creating an environment for high engagement and commitment.

As employees the more we can align our work to that which gives us a sense of meaning and purpose, the more energised and fulfilled we will be at work. We easily recognise people with passion; they exude positive energy compared to people who are just going through the motions.

A purpose is something bigger than you, it's something you align with and commit to. Meaningful work can give you a sense of fulfilment and well-being. The clearer you are about your values and personal vision, the better choices you will make about the work you do and where you work.

Research findings show that joy stems from believing one's work is truly meaningful. Employees who believe their "company makes a positive societal contribution" and who feel "personally committed to achieving the company's vision and strategy" experience the most joy at work.[92]

Reflection

As a leader:

- How do you create a sense of purpose at work?

- Are your company's values and expected behaviours clearly stated?

    □ If so, how do you make sure these values and behaviours are lived in your team?

    □ If not, how do you clarify values and expected behaviours with your team?

As HR:

- What is your role in making sure all employees understand the vision and values in the company and that they are actually lived by top management?

Chapter 5

Learning and growing at work to build capability and confidence

> In this chapter, we look at the importance of ongoing learning and development in employee engagement, and how leaders can support employee development.

Rochelle's feedback to Nicholas

"That was a more rigorous exercise than I imagined", said Rochelle. "Defining everyone's roles and how they contribute, as well as agreeing on the performance measures, took a while!"

"So how did you go about it?", asked Nicholas.

"I followed your process", said Rochelle. "At our weekly team meeting we listed all the roles and associated tasks and projects and allocated those to team members. We took people's strengths into account as well as the work they felt they would most like to be part of.

"I asked everyone to write a draft as per your template, then at the next meeting each person presented his or her role, objectives and performance measures to the team. The team made suggestions, especially on how the work contributed to our purpose and on the performance measures.

"Some people were very ambitious regarding their performance measures so we made them a bit more realistic. I also asked each person to reflect on their skill levels in relation to any new tasks they were taking on. We made sure each person's role is doable and that the work is evenly spread and appropriate for the person's level of seniority. We ticked off all the projects on our list and made sure everything was covered.

"So now everyone is clear on their roles. The core roles are essentially the same but everyone has something new; some work has been moved around to be more in line with people's strengths and where they want to contribute. I now have everything in place for performance reviews later, as well for my one-on-one meetings with team members. At our weekly team meetings, each person will present an update on their area of the business and we have plans to set up a visual display of results which we can update monthly. "I really think we are in a good space!"

"That is great progress", said Nicholas. "Here is your next challenge: we now need to think about skills development for your team. Have you given any thought to how team members, including you, will grow and develop, professionally and personally? How will your team keep up with new developments in their field and how will they be able to succeed in their new roles?"

"I hadn't given that much thought", said Rochelle, "apart from a marketing conference coming up later in the year. Yes, it's the next logical topic to address".

Ongoing learning and development is essential

As leaders, our role is to help bring out the best in people and support our team members' growth and development so that they experience success at work and the team achieves its goals. Nothing makes a person feel better about work than feeling highly successful and valued.

People only feel confident in taking on new challenges when they believe they have the skills and capabilities to do the job. As leaders we must ensure there is ongoing coaching and skills development so that collectively we are able to meet our current and future job requirements.

Employees generally rate opportunities to learn and grow as a high priority; they look for and stay with companies that offer great development opportunities. People want support to develop the skills they need to be successful at work, especially considering the massive technological changes they are facing. Many employees feel unprepared for Industry 4.0. They face the prospect of skills becoming obsolete, many current jobs disappearing and new jobs evolving, due to automation. They are looking to their employers to help them develop skills for the future, including "soft" skills such as complex problem solving, innovation and the social skills required for collaboration across the various work functions. These skills will be more important as jobs change and evolve.[93]

People generally want to expand their knowledge and skills so that they are able to achieve success at work and contribute in a meaningful way, and they are looking to their managers to support them. Employee growth and development is also important to the management of the company; we all want employees who have the skills to step up to complex challenges.

Looking ahead: Skills millennials expect they will need[94]

Technology is increasingly taking over routine tasks, so according to Deloitte's *Millennial Survey,* employees will be spending more time on creative, "human", and value-added work. In this scenario, skills mentioned by Millennials and Gen Z as being important are:

- interpersonal skills;
- emotional intelligence, especially self-confidence and personal engagement;
- ethics/integrity;
- critical thinking;
- innovation/creativity;
- communication;
- leadership;
- finance and economics;
- languages;
- having a global mindset; and
- analytical skills.

As managers, we need to be more creative in how we develop people, make better use of the workplace as a place to learn, and step up as coaches to our people.

"If you think training is expensive, try ignorance."

—Peter Drucker

The Development Plan

The starting point for focused and value-adding development is the Development Plan.

Here are the key steps to follow:

Firstly, identify the knowledge and skills each employee needs to be successful in their role. This list will include the categories listed below:

- Specific functional/technical skills to do the job well, e.g. mechatronics or accounting etc.
- Generic skills required in the role, e.g.:
  - problem solving;
  - judgement and decision-making;
  - process improvements;
  - business acumen;
  - assertiveness;
  - self-development;
  - stress management;
  - communication;
  - emotional intelligence; and
  - collaboration and team skills.
- Specific behaviours required to support the company's values, e.g.:
  - customer-centricity;
  - integrity;

- □ innovation; and
- □ respect.

- Leadership skills if the employee is in a management, team leader or project leader role, e.g.:
  - □ clarifying roles, goals and performance standards;
  - □ planning and organising;
  - □ monitoring performance;
  - □ performance reviews;
  - □ team problem solving and decision making;
  - □ enhancing employee engagement;
  - □ coaching;
  - □ selecting team members;
  - □ giving useful feedback;
  - □ leading team meetings;
  - □ communication and information sharing; and
  - □ developing team members' skills.

It's a good exercise to ask each employee to create a list of required competencies for their own jobs and bring it to the development plan discussion; this way you can see how people view their roles. As the manager you can make any required amendments and enhance their understanding of what "great" looks like.

Secondly, once these skills have been identified, you as the manager and the employee need to agree on the employee's current skill levels. You can use a simple rating such as Expert, Competent, Not Yet Competent.

The third step is to agree on how the skill gaps will be closed. As far as possible, "bake" learning into the daily work and use a variety of development approaches. With the pace of change in the workplace, we all need to be learning daily and the 70:20:10 approach is a good guideline to use.

How to apply the 70:20:10 principle in learning and development

Learning at work is everyone's responsibility; we all have knowledge to share and we all have skills and knowledge gaps. If we're curious, we'll learn every day at work by asking questions or doing our own research. We learn so we are competent in our present role as well as to prepare for our future roles, and we make use of the following ways to learn:

70% of development comes from work experiences

If you look back on your own career and what contributed the most to your development, you will most likely conclude that you grew the most through challenging work experiences, especially the ones at the edge of your comfort zone and skill set. Taking on a stretch project with new challenges and requiring new mindsets and skills will increase your capability and confidence, as well as expand your comfort zone moving forward.... provided of course the stretched comfort zone does not lead to failure and doesn't break our confidence.

So 70% of a development plan should be based on challenging and complex assignments and new experiences at work to foster learning. Some of these assignments will come about through new jobs, dealing with a crisis, trying a new approach, improving a process, joining a project team, working at a supplier, or addressing a new business opportunity. The principle is, we use work to learn.
A manager's role is to encourage a culture of investigation and curiosity; encourage people to take on new projects as learning experiences, and throughout the project ask questions, search the Internet for information, consult with experts where possible, and create small experiments to explore and validate ideas.

20% of learning comes from reflection and feedback

Both reflection and feedback are required for the full benefits of workplace experiences to be harvested. Bosses, mentors, coaches and peers can all assist our learning and development by being our sounding boards and helping us to gain new insights from our experiences at work.

It is also up to each employee to ask for feedback, test their thinking, exchange ideas or ask for advice. Through reflecting on experiences, we can challenge our assumptions, do some reality checks, identify what worked and what did not work, and assess what we could do differently. We also have the opportunity to shine a light on our blind spots through feedback. All of this is a crucial part of learning.

Without this ongoing debriefing of experiences, we may not consciously identify what we should do more or less of, and may continue to make the same mistakes thinking we are doing the right thing.

> **In practice:** As a coach, I often set up feedback sessions with the manager of the person being coached to reflect on strengths and areas of development. The reaction of the coachee is often, "But why didn't anyone tell me this years ago?" As managers, never underestimate the importance of your coaching and feedback role.

10% of our development will come from formal training, e-learning, courses, conferences and seminars

Formal training is useful for quickly sharing key knowledge and concepts, as well as doing some skill building. Training should replicate the real situation as closely as possible to assist in the transfer of skills from the classroom to the workplace. Many production training facilities, for example, use the same equipment people will use on the production line, or computer-based simulations and business games can be used for business strategy training. In leadership development or customer centricity training, role plays of typical situations help people to learn what works and does not work. Use training programmes that incorporate tools and experiential practice sessions for the greatest return on the time and money spent. These can include:

- group discussions on typical scenarios a person may face in their role;

- case studies to provide real life examples and engage all participants in sharing their views;

- role plays for interpersonal skills training or negotiation training; and

- games are also powerful for highlighting team dynamics and often lead to rich learnings.

In terms of presenting key concepts and theoretical models, ensure that these are presented in a user-friendly way; simple, short and visual is best, using infographics for example.

Training courses also need to allow time for participants to reflect on how they will use the knowledge back at the workplace and to list some key actions they will take. Consider providing performance support in the form of simple yet powerful checklists to help people apply what they have learned.

Other approaches could include formal study, participating in online courses or reading articles.

Putting 70:20:10 into practice

Formal training, workplace experiences and coaching and mentoring need to work together and support each other so that the learning can be integrated. For example, Leonard, a young engineer, has a need to develop his problem solving, judgement and decision-making skills as he has come up with some badly flawed recommendations recently. Applying the 70:20:10 principle, you as his manager agree on the following development approach with him:

- Leonard needs to complete the e-learning module on root cause analysis.

- He must develop a problem solving template consisting of key questions to ask when solving a technical problem and run this by you.

- You need to allocate Leonard three technical problems to investigate, using the template he developed.

- Shafeeka, a highly experienced engineer, will check in regularly with Leonard and give guidance where needed.

- Leonard will present his findings to you and Shafeeka, along with his recommendations.

- You will both test his logic and rationale through questions and give feedback.

- Leonard will present the results of his investigation at the quality meeting and take questions from your peers and other engineers.

- After the meeting you will debrief Leonard on the process he followed, lessons learned and how these will be applied going forward.

By following a thorough development process, you have empowered Leonard and no doubt increased his engagement at work as he experiences successes instead of humiliating failures. Having invested this time in Leonard, you will be able to let him work more independently as he will need less coaching from you on this topic. In addition, you have acknowledged Shafeeka as an expert which will increase her engagement at work. You have also improved the quality of work presented by your team which is good for your reputation. Everyone wins!

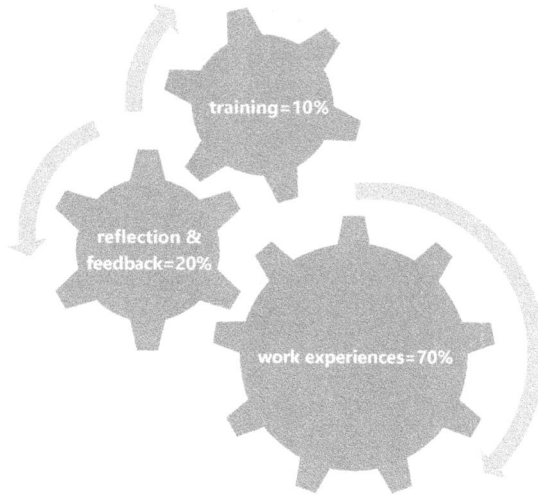

Figure 12: The 70:20:10 Principle

Leadership development

By now I am sure you are starting to see the huge impact that leadership has on employee engagement, so leadership development is absolutely essential.

The first step is a clear definition by top management of what you expect of a good leader in your company. This can be defined for first-line management, middle management and top management, as each plays a different role.

These competencies include skills such as EQ, social and interpersonal skills, coaching and people development, decision-making, performance management, planning and organising, leading meetings, business acumen, innovation and process improvement, quality management and so on. For more senior management, ability in strategic thinking and change management will also be important.

These definitions should be in your performance management documentation and leaders should be evaluated at least every year against these leadership competencies and skills gaps identified.

Ideally the Learning and Development specialists should be able to access data from the Performance Management system about the trends regarding strengths and areas where development is needed for each level of management as well as for individual managers.

For each group, you can set up relevant development to address the development needs identified, following the 70:20:10 principle.

70% of a leader's development could include experiences such as benchmarking trips, action learning assignments in a cross-functional team, implementing new processes, leading a project team and so on.

20% of a leader's development will come from coaching and mentoring, as well as feedback from their team or a 360 assessment. Many leaders are unaware of how their work makes a difference in the lives of their employees. In your one-on-one meetings with team members, at a team meeting, or at a teambuilding workshop, it is worthwhile asking what you do that is the most and the least helpful to the team, as well as what employees would like from you as their leader.

10% of the development can come from in-house workshops customised to your needs, business school programmes, e-learning and online courses.

Ways to increase the impact of leadership development programmes

Top management must:

- be actively involved in defining the leadership competencies;
- nominate candidates to participate in leadership development;
- set up action learning assignments;
- mentor project teams;
- show their support by opening leadership development programmes and highlighting the need for the development;

- ensure resources are available to offer top quality development programmes to the leadership group; and

- actively participate themselves in leadership development programmes.

Leadership development supports your talent management processes

Based on your succession plan, at each level of leadership you will have identified your top talent by evaluating them against a set of criteria, such as:

- performance ratings over the past three years;
- exposure to other divisions within the company;
- successful project implementation;
- formal qualifications; and
- development activities undertaken.

Your top talent then needs leadership development that will prepare them for the next level of management.

At the individual contributor level you will also have identified employees who show potential for leadership, and programmes can be developed to prepare this group for leadership roles.

Talent management done well is also a great motivator for your leadership groups.

A growth mindset is required for learning and development to happen[95]

For employees to learn and develop, a growth mindset is required. Stanford's Carol Dweck spent her career studying failure and how people react to failure. She noted that some people avoided a challenge while others thrived when confronted by a challenge. Her conclusion was people have either a "fixed mindset" or a "growth mindset".

■ People with a fixed mindset dislike challenges and failure because they believe that talent is a fixed thing that you're born with — or not. Those who have a fixed mindset focus on the things they cannot do and avoid new challenges.

■ Those who thrive under challenge she identified as having a "growth mindset". Those with a growth mindset view challenges as an opportunity to deepen their talents. They believe that challenges can be overcome with effort and good guidance.

As a leader, we need to encourage and support people to take on new challenges as a way to learn and grow; we need to move employees away from "I can't do it" towards an "I can't do it yet" mindset.

Real gains require a personal growth mindset, where the individual is motivated and curious to learn, apply and improve, supported by an organisational culture which understands that failure is an intrinsic part of growth. When we apply a new skill for the first time, we may not get it right, so ongoing support for learning is essential.

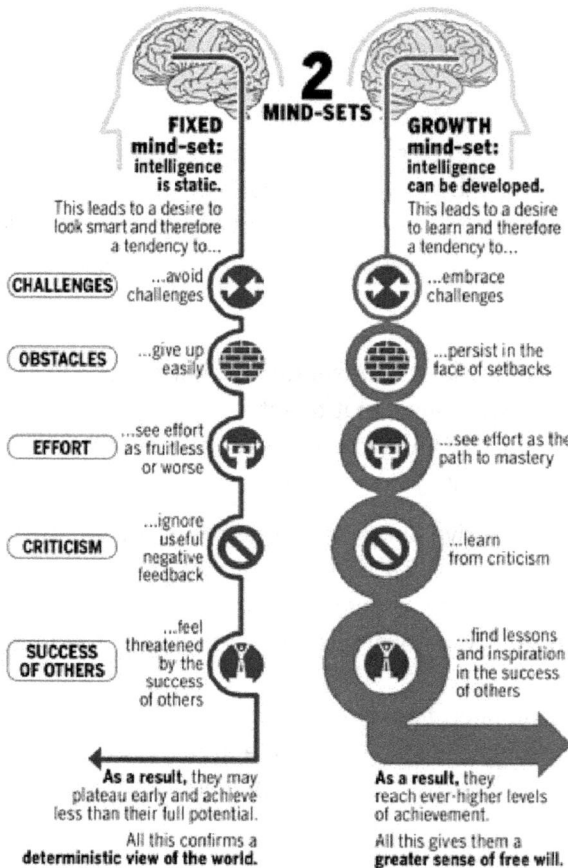

Figure 13: Carol Dweck: "Fixed mindsets" or "growth mindsets"[96]

Think back to Leonard in our example above: he adopted the growth mindset and agreed to his development plan, but as a young person at the beginning of his career, maybe it was easier.

Will the development approach used with Leonard work with a senior person? Learning can make us feel vulnerable; we have to admit that we are not skilled in something. We may feel we should know these things and resist development activities or trying out new behaviours. It requires courage as a senior person to embrace learning, but your willingness to be vulnerable, say you too need ongoing development, and involve yourself in learning and growing will send a positive message to your team about the importance of ongoing development. With the rapidly changing environment of business, learning must be a high priority for all levels in the organisation, so tell your team if you are working with a coach, participating in leadership development activities, or attending a conference or a workshop. Learning must become the new normal for everyone, requiring that we step out of our comfort zones into a growth zone.

"The comfort zone is the great enemy to creativity; moving beyond it necessitates intuition, which in turn configures new perspectives and conquers feats."

—Dan Stevens

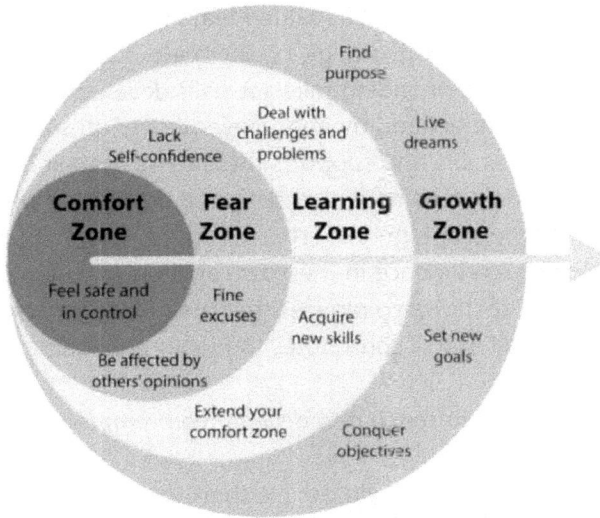

Figure 14: Leaving the comfort zone

The leader as coach

Being a leader in the role of coach requires us to understand people's strengths and what work feels meaningful to them, move them into roles to leverage these, and coach them to be successful and build on these strengths.[97]

People generally, and Millennials especially, don't want an old-style "command and control" boss. They want their manager to coach and develop them in order to help them to accelerate their personal and professional growth. Ongoing feedback and coaching conversations make an important difference to how people feel about their work.[98]

> Businesses that orient performance management systems around basic human needs for psychological engagement – such as positive workplace relationships, frequent recognition, ongoing performance conversations and opportunities for personal development – get the most out of their employees.[99]

The best leaders treat people as valued team members by coaching and mentoring them, giving them attention, support and encouragement, and providing relevant skills development. These managers try to understand their employees' strengths and what motivates each person, and supports them to be at their best at work through encouragement, coaching and doing their best to remove any barriers to high performance. In this way, they build their employees' confidence in their own abilities and ultimately their success at work. It shows employees that their manager wants them to succeed and all of this contributes to higher engagement at work.

The skills you need to coach and develop your employees

As a coach, your role is to help people think through problems and challenges, as well as to offer your perspective and guidance when needed. Coaching helps to unlock people's potential to maximise their own performances. It is about raising self-awareness and personal responsibility, and helping people to learn, rather than teaching them.

> "The quality of everything we do depends on the quality of the thinking we do first."
>
> **—Nancy Kline**

All of the practices mentioned in Chapter 2 form the basis for coaching to take place; a sense of trust, respect, belonging and support are essential in a coaching relationship as we need the person we are coaching to be open and reflective, to speak freely about what is on their mind, and to say where they are having difficulties.

In addition, there are some specific skills needed to coach well:

- **Powerful questions and active listening** to stimulate reflection and insights in the person you are coaching.

    "If I had an hour to solve a problem and my life depended on the solution, I would spend the first 55 minutes determining the proper question to ask, for once I know the proper question, I could solve the problem in ess than five minutes."

    —Albert Einstein

? **Powerful questions:**

- stimulate a reflective conversation;
- are thought-provoking;
- surface underlying assumptions;
- invite creativity and new possibilities
- generate energy and forward movement; and
- channel attention and focus inquiry.

Active listening

This is listening to understand rather than listening to reply. It includes summarising, identifying feelings and assumptions, and picking up on themes.

Questions and active listening encourage reflection and ownership, but as the person's manager, you will have to decide when to offer your perspective and guidance.

Good coaching will leave the person with some new insights, feeling encouraged, energised, acknowledged and knowing what to do next.

Task-focused coaching

Employees appreciate regular meetings with their managers. The best leaders conduct regular check-ins with each team member where they agree expectations and priorities, give feedback, suggest changes or alternative ways to proceed, or provide required information. Providing clarity on goals and priorities is an important role for a leader. Clarity regarding what success looks like and how best to proceed are important conversations and are an important part of a leader's role. These meetings actually save time for the leader as errors and queries are reduced and employees are empowered to move ahead without frequent check-ins with the leader.

Regular meetings, coaching and consistent feedback improve employee engagement and performance. Employees who meet regularly with their leader feel more supported and recognised, and that their leader cares about their well-being, success and development.

Using coaching skills in these one-on-one meetings will turn them into great value-adding conversations. Two useful frameworks you can use are:

The Kolb Learning Cycle[100]

This framework is useful for debriefing situations and identifying learnings.

Step 1: Concrete experience

For example, imagine your team member tells you she led a project team meeting that went very badly. She is upset and needs to make sense of what happened and how to deal with a similar situation in the future. So how to coach her through this experience?

Concrete Experience
(doing/having an experience)

Active Experimentation
(planning/trying out what you have learned)

Reflective Observation
(reviewing/reflecting on the experience)

Abstract Conceptualisation
(concluding/learning from the experience)

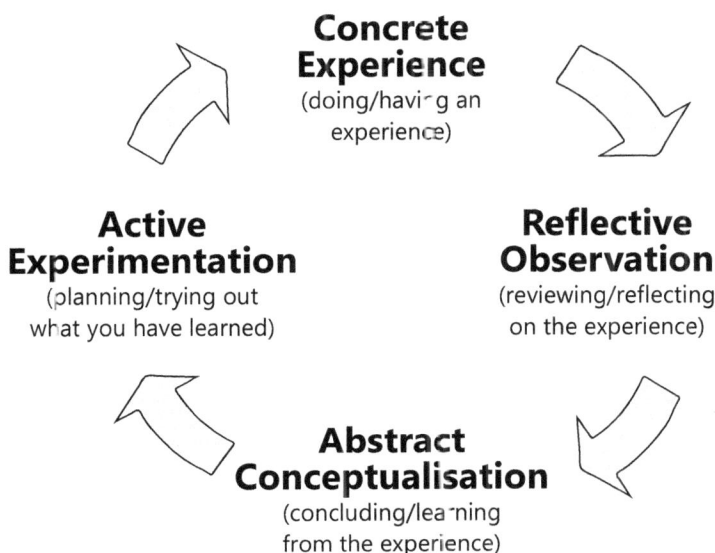

Figure 15: The Kolb Learning Cycle

STEP 2: Reflective observation

For the experience you need to coach the person through, ask the person to reflect on what happened:

- What happened in the meeting?
    - What successes did you experience?
    - What problems or difficulties did you experience?
    - How did you react to the problem situations?
    - Who was involved?
    - What did you do?
- What assumptions did you make about what was happening?
    - What were you saying to yourself in the midst of these challenges?
    - What thoughts were running through your mind?

□   How did that affect your actions?

□   What did you want to achieve?

STEP 3: Learning from the experience

Reflection is all about getting into deeper thinking, and questions are the stimulus to help get us there.

- What actions of yours worked well? What helped you achieve success?
- What actions of yours didn't work? What contributed to problems?
- What skills did you use?
- What was the impact of your actions?
- How can I use this experience going forward?
- How does this experience relate to other similar situations I have been in and what can I learn from this experience?
- What can you learn:
  - □   from this person or situation?
  - □   from what went wrong?
  - □   from what went well?
- What does all of this mean to you? What message are you getting from this?
- How has this situation been an asset? Is there a positive side to this problem?
- What's taking shape? What are you thinking and feeling now?
- What new insights are emerging?
- What's been your major learning, insight, or discovery so far? What can you learn from what's happened?

Allow these questions and similar types of questions to open up a broader base of thinking. Help the person think about what they can take from their experiences and how they can apply the lessons to other situations.

■   Look for generalisations and similar patterns.

STEP 4: Gain the learning

Ask these questions that will help the person make decisions going forward:

■   If this situation happened again, what would you do differently?

■   How can you use the insights gained for future situations?

Concluding the discussion

The debrief: If the person needs to take any actions to remedy the situation, ask the following questions:

■   What needs your immediate attention going forward?

■   What are your choices?

■   What can you do that could help shift this situation?

■   What possibilities do you now see?

■   What motivates (or pushes) you to solve the problem? How energised are you to master this type of issue?

■   What support do you need in taking the next steps?

■   What challenges might come your way and how might you meet them?

■   If you could only take the one option that you believe would add the most value, what would it be?

■   Where do you want to put your best effort?

■   What will you do, when?

Reflection leads to greater success

When we reflect with people in this way in a safe space, we will help others come to a significant understanding of past experiences that can set them up to succeed in future situations. The alternative is to keep making the same mistakes. The ability to be disciplined enough to practice self-reflection holds the key to our future success.

The GROW Model[101]

This is an excellent framework to use when you are assigning a new role or project to an employee, or if you are reviewing progress on existing projects. Expectations are clarified, obstacles are discussed and agreements are reached in terms of how the person will proceed.

GROW stands for Goal, (current) Reality, Options and Way forward

Let's say you're reviewing progress on a project with an employee and the employee is a bit anxious and really wants to be successful. To clarify expectations and the way forward with the project, start the coaching conversation as follows:

Step 1 of the GROW Model: Goal questions

These questions get the person thinking through the purpose and aims of the project. The discussion might include the end goal or purpose of the project, or shorter-term milestones or progress goals along the way:

- What is our picture of success?
- What is the ultimate aim of this project?
- What impact should it have?
- How does this project support the purpose of the team?
- Who is the "customer" and how will we meet his or her needs?

Step 2 of the GROW Model: What is the Current Reality?

- What is the current situation in terms of the action taken so far?
- What are the results and effects of previously taken actions?
- What successes are we seeing?
- What is limiting our progress?
- What problems are we encountering?
    - What is happening that should not be happening?
    - What are the reasons for these problems occurring?

Step 3 of the GROW Model: What are your Options?

- What options or possible courses of action can we identify?
- What are the pros and cons of each option?
- What seems to be the best course of action?

Step 4 of the GROW Model: What will you do (Way Forward)?

- How will we proceed?
- What actions do you believe will make the biggest difference?
- What must we change in order to achieve our goals?
- What is the plan of action for implementation of the identified steps?
- Do we anticipate any future obstacles?
- Whose support do you need?
- How confident are you that you will be able to implement this plan?
- What progress feedback is required?

This kind of clarity and support is important for people, especially less experienced employees; people want to know what success will look like, how their job performance will be evaluated, how their jobs support team and organisational goals, and if they are going about the task in the best way. Knowing what is expected of me is an important factor in my personal engagement and success. This goes beyond what a job description can supply; employees want managers to provide them with clarity and support.

Peer coaching

There may be occasions when an employee has taken on a new role or project and needs advice on how to proceed. Generally teams are very diverse so there is a large amount of knowledge and skills to draw on. This is when peer coaching is a great way to support someone.

It works as follows:

- A 60-90 minute meeting is set up.
- A list of people who can give useful input is drawn up and invited to the meeting. This invitation could come from the person's manager.
- A facilitator is selected.
- The meeting then proceeds as follows:
  - The employee presents his/her problem or ideas (with no interruptions) for 5-7 minutes.
  - The colleagues ask questions to explore the issue from all angles (using rounds, i.e. each person gets a chance to explore the issue by going one by one to each person around the table) for 10-12 minutes.
  - The colleagues share their impressions (rounds) for 10-12 minutes.
  - The employee responds by summarising and giving his/her own views for 5-7 minutes.
  - We mind map the issue with possible solutions (open discussion, facilitator leads the mind mapping exercise) for 10-15 minutes.

- ☐ The issue holder chooses the most helpful ideas and solutions (5-7 minutes).

- ☐ Closing and evaluation of the meeting (rounds) for 5-7 minutes.

This approach is great for sharing knowledge and experience, and always results in people getting a much deeper insight into the issue as well as many new ideas on how to proceed.

Feedback

Most employees are keen to know how they are doing and if they need to do anything differently.

This is where feedback comes in, which is most useful if it is specific. Be careful of generalisations or assumptions, and focus on specific behaviours and their consequences. So instead of saying, "I find you to be irresponsible", rather say:

Behaviour: I have noticed that you often hand in reports a day or two late.

Consequence: This delays the information I must distribute to people who attend the Financial Review meeting.

I would prefer that you plan your work so you can meet the deadlines agreed.

Problem solving: What is the reason for these reports not being in on time?

Agreements: So let's agree then...

Concrete feedback like this is far more useful to employees. High-level feedback, for example about personal traits ("You're a great team player" or "You lack attention to detail"), is not helpful because it's too vague and people don't know what they must either continue to do or what they must do differently. Concrete feedback about behaviour helps people to be clear about what they should and should not do going forward.

When you have to deal with poor performance

There will be times when people mess up or behave badly, and we as the manager will need to have a conversation with the employee. Any conversation about poor performance must have the intention of improving performance in the future. It is not an opportunity for us to express anger and frustration; rather do that in private somewhere else. Blame and criticism lead to defensive behaviour, so we need to be calm and rational when we have these conversations. Be assertive but not aggressive; maintain the person's self-esteem and don't accuse, blame, judge, label or think the worst of the person. The person did not want to fail and you have to work with them after this meeting, so follow these steps to help turn it into a productive discussion.

■ State the purpose of the meeting and say what is concerning you:

□ State your concern factually, e.g. you have been late three times this week; the figures you gave me were incorrect; a customer complained.

□ State the impact/consequences of this.

■ Ask for the person's point of view/feedback: What led up to this?

□ Ask open questions.

□ Listen.

■ Ask the person how this can be prevented in the future:

□ What solutions can the person offer?

■ Present your views:

□ Say if you agree or disagree with the solutions put forward.

□ Offer alternative solutions if needed.

□ Refer to company values or operational requirements for rationale.

■ Resolve points of disagreement:

□ Ask if you can support in some way.

- Agree on a plan going forward.
- Affirm the person's value to the team.

Coaching for confidence

For people to take on new challenges, projects and roles, they need the confidence that they can succeed. In coaching conversations, it's important to ask people what their confidence levels are when facing a challenging task. If they feel they will not succeed, then ask them to list all their beliefs about why they will not succeed and ask them to examine these. Try to separate the "real" issues (e.g. it is an untested approach) from limiting assumptions (e.g. they will not cooperate with me).

Some assumptions when we look at them we can probably recognise as untrue. Other fears may be real. So we need to agree with the employee how to handle these and where you or others can support them.

Over time, successes build confidence, so as leaders, we need to set people up for success.

The performance review discussion

As an engaging leader, your focus will be on frequent coaching conversations and informal check-ins with your team. So when your company is looking for a rating of each employee for salary and bonus purposes, there should be no surprises for any of your team members.

At their performance review, you may ask an employee to reflect on the year under review in terms of their achievements and the impact of these, as well as projects that did not go so well and the lessons learned. Ask them to review their growth and development and what they have learned about their strengths.

It is also important to reflect on the company values and behaviours and to what extent they are living those. If it is an annual review, it's probably time to talk about projects and roles they would like to grow into.

Then it's time for you to give feedback on your views of their performance and your overall assessment and rating. Mention their strengths and what is needed to develop those further, as well as the person's impact on the team's performance. It is important to affirm the person so that they leave motivated to perform well and to work on their areas of development.

A challenge for all employees

Learning and growing our job-related skills as well as our personal skills is a responsibility we all need to take seriously if we want to be successful at work and make a contribution. The opportunities for growth and development are all around us in the form of people with expertise and insights, the Internet, new challenges, coaches and mentors, workshops and seminars. To develop our personal qualities, we also need to be open to feedback and to learn new approaches. If we harvest the learning opportunities around us through being curious and finding out more, we will soon be experts in what we do.

The Importance of the Leader in employee development

Employees are more engaged and inspired when their leader is committed to their growth. Being a coach and mentor to people is a very rewarding role and you will experience the loyalty and appreciation from your team.

Summary

Summary
☐ —
☐ —
☐ —

Engaged employees care about the quality of their work and to meet high standards, employees need skills. With the rapid changes taking place in the workplace, learning and development can no longer be an occasional activity; they need to take place on an ongoing basis. Managers need to think more about the kinds of skills required for top performance and identify ways to develop these skills, using a variety of approaches. This should come together in an employee's development plan.

Companies need to offer relevant skills training programmes addressing functional skills as well as business, personal and leadership skills. Employees need to play an active role in their own development by making use of all the resources available to them at work, such as workshops and seminars, coaching and mentoring, taking on new projects and roles, e-learning and so on.

The manager's role as a coach is becoming increasingly important as a way to build skills, confidence and self-insight in employees. Employees want to know their manager is supportive of their development and the ability to coach well is a skill all managers need to acquire.

Chapter 6

The Leaders Role in Employee Engagement

In this chapter, we focus on the leader's role in the engagement of their people, the concept of Conscious Leadership, leadership styles and important personal qualities required of leaders.

"Let us all be the leaders we wish we ˉad."

— **Simon Sinek**, *Leaders Eat Last: Why Some Teams Pull Together and Others Don't*

Rochelle and Nicholas discuss leadership

"Our final session", said Rochelle. "What more is there to talk about?"

"A final reflection on your leadership role". said Nicholas.

"But that's all we've spoken about", said Rochelle, "are you saying there is more for me to do?"

"Yes, it's time to think holistically about your role as the manager of this department, as well as some of the personal qualities you need to be a success in a leadership role."

The manager's impact on engagement

A well-known observation from the Gallup Organisation is that people join companies but leave managers! Managers have a big impact on the everyday experience of employees; they account for at least 70% of variance in employee engagement scores.[102]

You will have noticed throughout the preceding chapters how crucial the manager's role is in employee engagement. People want to work for managers who support them, give them work in line with their strengths and passion, develop and engage them, and care about them both as employees and people.

Great companies are built by great leaders. Leaders' decisions and behaviours and the cultures these create play an important role in the engagement of any employee. Some workplace cultures motivate employees and lead to high performance. Others are toxic and drain employees' motivation, leaving people feeling discouraged and low in energy.

According to Gallup's research, poor management costs the U.S. between $960 billion and $1.2 trillion per year in productivity lost to disengagement. Globally, the cost approaches $7 trillion, or 9% to 10% of the world's GDP.[103]

Senior leaders need to be the champions of employee engagement; if they do that well, it's more likely that middle and first-line managers will support and sustain the behaviours and practices that lead to high engagement. Senior leadership's involvement and interest in employee engagement sends signals to all levels of leadership that engagement is a high priority for the organisation, and that leadership must accept accountability for employee engagement so that the company is successful in the long term.

Most companies have defined values and behaviours for their employees, such as excellence of work, quality, innovation, customer experience, collaboration, integrity and so on, and have communicated these expectations. Plus, there are stretch targets for employees in terms of production, market share, profit, as well as some employee metrics such as attendance, labour turnover and training.

Once organisations have clarified the goals of the company and their expectations of their employees, the missing piece is often how they will achieve the active support of their employees to help make this happen. How will they unlock employees' drive and energy to want to go the extra mile? How do leaders establish an organisational culture in which engagement can thrive? How do leaders create an environment that attracts, retains and develops employees? This leads us to a reflection on our leadership brand and what we expect of our leaders. Teams are more autonomous and may be dispersed geographically, so in this complex and fast-changing world, the old "command and control" style of leadership is fast becoming irrelevant. One person simply cannot have all the answers! Employees today expect their managers to coach them to succeed at work, to value them as people, and to have real relationships with them. Management is key to every aspect of the workplace.

What is expected of leaders?

As we can see, in this rapidly changing world, people want their leaders to provide vision, direction, stability and support, and to be people who their employees respect.[104] A leader's role is to inspire and enable others to do their best work and ensure the business is successful in the long run.

However the qualities that made us stand out and be promoted to leadership are not always the ones that will make us great leaders. Being a strong technical specialist with personal drive and energy may not mean we know how to inspire and engage others. As leaders, we need to think through our leadership beliefs and practices and ask ourselves how best we add value to our organisations and the people we lead. Leadership requires a new mindset and skillset.

■ Are you more of a manager or more of a leader?

As business leaders, we need to be good at both management and leadership. We need a vision, as well as the ability to execute our vision and achieve results. To inspire and engage people at work we need to go beyond the traditional management role and be visionary, form bonds with the people we lead, and inspire them by helping them to find meaning, purpose and connection at work.

In our leadership role, we:

- lead and care for people;
- have a vision for something better – we want to make a positive difference to something important;
- provide direction;
- focus on the big picture;
- are able to influence and inspire people;
- challenge the status quo; and
- focus on the horizon – we see the future approaching.

In our management role, we:

- manage resources, which includes people;
- plan;
- organise;
- measure/monitor;
- improve current processes; and
- focus on the bottom-line, with a short-term focus.

The leadership roles and the management roles need to work in harmony, as we can see from this quote:

> "Work without vision is drudgery. Vision without work is dreaming. Work plus vision-this is destiny."
>
> **—Gordon B. Hinckley**

> "Anyone who manages people has a leadership responsibility. Formal authority is never sufficient to gain enthusiasm from those to be managed. An essential part of the manager's job is to enlist the full cooperation of those she leads, shifting their motivation from external compliance to internal commitment. Thus great leadership is a necessary condition for great management."
>
> **—Fred Kofman,** *Conscious Business*

The leader's intention

Vision and connection with people are the starting points to inspire employees.

Employees want to know: Am I working hard to further my leader's career, am I working hard to develop my skills and further my own career, or am I working hard to make a contribution to something important? Leaders can be more ego-driven and personally ambitious or more contribution-driven, and how employees interpret their leader's intention has a big influence on their engagement.

Great leaders understand that leadership goes beyond self-interest. This does not mean we do not take care of our own interests, but our intention is less on personal gain and more on the long-term benefits for others.

The most effective leaders are those who are motivated by purpose and service to people. They are more able to inspire people to achieve extraordinary levels of engagement, creativity and performance through vision, and through finding ways for people to achieve a sense of meaning, human connectedness, success and happiness at work. People who can see that their collective efforts contribute something positive to society, the company, the customer and the people working in the team are more engaged and feel greater trust and loyalty to the leader.

> "If management views workers not as valuable individuals but as tools to be discarded when no longer needed, then employees will regard the firm as nothing more than a machine for issuing pay checks, with no other value or meaning. Under such conditions it is difficult to do a good job, let alone enjoy one's work."
>
> **—Mihaly Csikszentmihalyi**

Leaders need to truly embrace the value of people and not merely see them as a commodity or a resource. This is what is meant by the term "Servant Leadership", a term used to describe visionary leaders who have the intention to make a positive difference.

■ Servant leadership: Robert Greenleaf

Servant leadership is a philosophy and practice of leadership, which was defined by Robert Greenleaf in the 1970s and has been supported by many leadership and management writers such as Simon Sinek, Ken Blanchard, Stephen Covey, Peter Block, Peter Senge, Max DePree and Margaret Wheatley.

Servant leadership emphasises the leader's role as steward of the company's resources: human, financial, technological, and so forth. It encourages leaders to serve others while staying focused on achieving results in line with the organisation's vision, mission and values.

Servant leaders achieve results for their organisations by giving priority attention to a purpose bigger than themselves. Leadership is not about me and personal gain – it is about the people and the organisation I lead. Decisions I make will be based on the long-term benefits for all.

Robert Greenleaf felt that the power-centred authoritarian leadership style was not working. The following statement by Greenleaf summarises his thinking:

> "The servant-leader is servant first... It begins with the natural feeling that one wants to serve, to serve first. Then conscious choice brings one to aspire to lead. That person is sharply different from one who is leader first, perhaps because of the need to assuage an unusual power drive or to acquire material possessions... The leader-first and the servant-first are two extreme types. Between them there are shadings and blends that are part of the infinite variety of human nature."
>
> **—Robert K. Greenleaf.**[105]

The servant leadership concept has evolved into Conscious Business and Conscious Leadership:

■ Conscious Business and Conscious Leadership

This is a philosophy of doing business in which the business sets itself a higher purpose than simply making a profit. This purpose is the difference the company is trying to make in the world. By focusing on its higher purpose, a business inspires, engages and energises all its stakeholders.

The focus is on the "Triple Bottom Line" where the aim of the business is to make a **profit** while providing value to **people** (employees, customer, suppliers and the community) and the **planet.**

Conscious businesses are created by visionary leaders who are committed to business as a force for good. Conscious leaders understand and embrace the vision and purpose of the business and focus on creating a culture, i.e. the values, principles and practices that support this.

A conscious business considers what is best for its employees as well as its customers, developing products and services that support their well-being.

As far back as 2013, a *Harvard Business Review* article showed companies that practice 'Conscious Capitalism' perform ten times better than their peers.[106]

Conscious Companies South Africa (https://www.consciouscompanies. co.za/) defines a Conscious Company as being led by a courageous and visionary leader who is deeply aware of his actions and the impact he has on all of his stakeholders.

"A Conscious Company is a transformational organisation. Its dominant ethos is:

- **Authenticity** – creates a brand and operating culture that is steeped in integrity

- **Purpose** – keeps its sights on a higher purpose that transcends the bottom line

- **Stakeholder Engagement** – is always conscious of the needs of all stakeholders including equity owners, staff, customers and communities

---

> - **Visionary Leadership** – the business is run by a conscious leader and fosters future visionary leaders
>
> - **Trust, Accountability, Ethics and Governance** – maintains the principles of a moral code
>
> - **Creativity & Innovation** – is progressive in its outlook, driving disruption and new methodologies
>
> - **Responsible Citizen** – always recognises and exceeds its obligation in the communities it operates in effecting social impact"

Full Spectrum Leadership[107]

A conscious leader with a vision of creating a sustainable business focusing on profit, people and planet will practice **Full Spectrum Leadership**, which simply means covering all the activities required for a successful and sustainable business.

Richard Barrett's *Full Spectrum Leadership* illustrates how we evolve as leaders. It describes all the aspects of leading and managing we must master if we are to fulfil our vision of a sustainable business contributing to something important.

Barrett's seven levels of leadership consciousness is a holistic view of the leadership role; to be successful as leaders, we need to master each level:

- Level 1 focuses on the survival and security of the organisation through strong operational and financial management.

- Level 2 looks at building relationships of trust and belonging.

- Level 3 aims to take the organisation's performance to levels of excellence through ongoing process improvements. This ensures the company remains competitive in its market.

These are the traditional management roles and many companies do not expect more of their leaders than this. Companies that do not progress beyond Level 3 are usually unable to inspire employees.

Visionary Leadership starts at Level 4:

- At Level 4, leaders make an internal values shift; their vision broadens and they want to develop and empower themselves and others. They work collaboratively to make a significant contribution to something beyond themselves. They then enter the Servant Leadership/Conscious Leadership space, where they are more able to inspire and engage others.

- At Level 5, the leader's focus is on collaboration and winning support for the vision.

- At Level 6 the focus is on partnerships, personal development, the development of others and the creation of a strong culture of ethics, integrity and contribution.

- At Level 7 the focus is on contribution and service to people and the planet.

Table 1: The Seven Levels of Leadership Consciousness

Levels of consciousness		Characteristics
7	Service	**Wisdom/Visionary**: Service to society, humanity and the planet. Focus on ethics, social responsibility, sustainability and future generations.
		Displays wisdom, compassion and humility.
6	Making a difference	**Mentor/Partner**: Strategic alliances and partnerships, servant leadership. Focus on employee fulfilment, and mentoring and coaching.
		Displays empathy and utilises intuition in decision-making.
5	Internal cohesion	**Integrator/Inspirer**: Strong cohesive culture and a capacity for collective action. Focus on vision, mission and values. Displays authenticity, integrity, passion and creativity.

Levels of consciousness		Characteristics
4	**Transformation**	**Facilitator/Influencer**: Empowerment, adaptability and continuous learning. Focus on personal growth, teamwork and innovation. Displays courage, responsibility, initiative, and accountability.
3	**Self-esteem**	**Manager/Organiser**: High performance systems and processes. Focus on strategy, performance, excellence, quality, productivity and efficiency. Displays pride in performance.
2	**Relationship**	**Relationship Manager/Communicator**: Employee recognition, open communication and conflict resolution. Creates employee and customer loyalty, and treats people with dignity.
1	**Survival**	**Financial Manager/Crisis Director**: Financial stability, organisational growth, and employee health and safety. Displays calmness in the face of chaos, and decisiveness in the midst of danger.

@ Take the free Values Assessment at the Barrett Values Centre to see what is most important to you:
https://www.valuescentre.com/our-products/products-individuals/personal-values-assessment-pva

"The true price of leadership is the willingness to place the needs of others above your own. Great leaders truly care about those they are privileged to lead and understand that the true cost of the leadership privilege comes at the expense of self-interest."

— **Simon Sinek**, *Leaders Eat Last: Why Some Teams Pull Together and Others Don't*

Leadership roles and skills

To be a Full Spectrum Leader and bring out the best in others, leaders need a range of leadership skills to meet the needs of the specific situation.

Daniel Goleman identified six leadership styles and skill sets leaders must be able to draw on, depending on the situation. Each set of skills is appropriate to specific situations and we cannot rely on only one or two skill sets if we are to be a Full Spectrum Leader. The most effective leaders know what is needed in each situation.[108]

1. **The Command Style:** A leader may need to use this autocratic approach on occasions. "Do-it-because-I-say-so". It is also known as the "My way or the highway" style. This may be appropriate in crisis situations or when drastic change is required. It is probably best suited to the survival issues of Level 1 on Barrett's model. This is when compliance and tight control and monitoring are needed. Orders must be followed unquestioningly.

    This style is problematic when over-used as it tends to include threats, frequent criticism and rare praise, which eventually erodes people's spirits and pride and satisfaction in their work. This is the least effective approach if used in situations other than a crisis; an autocratic and intimidating leader affects everyone's mood and engagement, team input is minimal, the climate spirals down and performance suffers.

    To use the commanding style well, a leader needs:

    - the drive to achieve;
    - the know-how to exert forceful direction in order to get better results;
    - initiative: the leader does not wait for situations to drive him/her, but rather takes forceful steps to get things done;

- emotional self-control and empathy to keep anger, impatience or contempt in check ("Be angry with the right person, in the right way, at the right time and for the right reason." – Aristotle); and

- to know when the situation needs a strong hand at the top and when to drop it.

Note to self: To what extent am I using this style and what has been the impact?

2. **Affiliative Leadership:** When this style and skills are used well, people feel valued and their feelings are considered. These skills are particularly needed from Level 2 upwards in Barrett's model; the leader works at building good relationships and harmony in the team. By connecting with people, by building trust and respect, and by offering emotional support during difficult times, these leaders build tremendous loyalty. People want to feel a sense of connection, belonging and inclusion, so this style is essential at all times and required even more when a leader needs to build morale, create harmony or repair broken trust. A supportive, trusting and non-controlling relationship with a supervisor and good co-worker relations encourages engagement.

A leader cannot rely only on this approach, however; if the leader places relationships, harmony and personal popularity as the priority, results can suffer, poor performance can go uncorrected and mediocrity may become the norm. Conflict is often avoided and people don't get the feedback they need to grow. The team may feel directionless.

This style works well in combination with the Visionary and Pace-Setting approaches.

To use this style well, the leader needs the skills of:

- listening;
- empathy;
- conflict resolution; and
- trust building.

Note to self: To what extent am I using this style and what has been the impact?

3. **Pace-setting Leadership:** This style and skills allow the leader to set high standards and expect excellence (faster, cheaper, better)! The focus is on results and continuous improvement. The leader leads by example, and will do the work him/herself if necessary. Poor performers are quickly identified and more is asked of them; if they don't rise to the occasion, the leader will take over and do it. There is an impatience with poor performers. This approach works well with competent, self-motivated and achievement-orientated people, where the challenges are big.

The down-side of pace-setting is that if it is over-used, people feel pushed too hard. Pace-setting leaders are often unclear about their requirements; people must just "know what to do". Morale drops when people are unsure and under pressure. People often feel the leader does not care about them as people and continuing high stress and pressure can be debilitating; the leader gets short-term results, but in the longer term, people become disengaged and uncreative.

Pace-setting skills include an:

- achievement drive, i.e. a personal need to achieve high standards; and
- initiative to seize opportunities.

Pace-setting is best used in combination with the Affiliative Style, with skills such as empathy, self-management and team skills. Otherwise these leaders simply apply pressure, become impatient, criticise, never recognise, and eventually destroy morale. Use with care!

> **Note to self:** To what extent am I using this style and what has been the impact?

4. **Participative Leadership:** Leaders use this style and skills to engage others in the decision-making process; they ask questions and listen, and their approach is collaborative and democratic. Their aim is to build trust, consensus and buy-in. This style works well when the team consists of highly competent individuals, the situation is complex and the leader is uncertain about what direction to take, or when the leader needs ideas from employees, e.g. how to achieve a goal or new ways of handling a situation. These leaders are facilitators and do not rely on position power.

The skills needed by a participative leader are:

■ listening: these leaders really do want to hear what people think so they make it safe for people to speak up and be honest and open; and

■ team building skills of collaboration, consensus, engagement, conflict resolution, diversity management and influencing skills.

A leader must be careful not to overuse this style; the outcome could be endless meetings and discussions with no decisions, causing delays and confusion and maybe escalating conflict. This approach is not appropriate:

■ with employees who are not able to give meaningful input; and

■ in a crisis when quick decisions are needed.

Note to self: To what extent am I using this style and what has been the impact?

5. **The Leader as Coach:** The leader makes time for conversations with employees about their personal growth, aspirations and career goals, and how to accomplish these. They discuss the employees' strengths and development needs, and they give feedback. The focus is on the person and their development and motivation; the leader tries to link daily work to the employee's strengths and long-term goals. As a coach, the leader delegates and gives challenging assignments to help develop people.

Coaching works best with employees who are motivated, show initiative and want development. Leaders must have the expertise and sensitivity necessary to coach, give feedback and delegate challenging assignments. Skills needed to coach include:

■ counselling;

■ creating rapport;

■ giving guidance and advice in the best interests of the employee; and

■ developing talent.

If coaching and feedback is done badly, this can lead to apathy and fear; the delegation can look like micro-managing and a focus on short-term goals may make people feel like they are just being used to get an extra job done.

> **Note to self:** To what extent am I using this style and what has been the impact?

6. **Visionary Leadership:** The leader gains people's support by clarifying the big picture, setting standards, elucidating how their work supports the company's direction and strategy, and explaining how they are making a difference to something important. Asking these questions is key:

    ■ Where are we going?

    ■ Why is this important in the bigger scheme of things?

    ■ Who benefits from our success?

    ■ What are our challenges?

This creates shared goals and a sense of pride, and people understand why their jobs matter.

In an era of rapid change, vision becomes even more important as a means of providing clarity, focus and direction. The route may change but if the destination remains clear, people have some sense of stability and clarity. Vision gives us the purpose behind what we do and how we contribute to something important. This energises people as it makes work more meaningful.

Leaders of the most successful organisations have clearly articulated their vision, even though there may be massive short-term uncertainty.

This leadership skill is essential when a clear direction is needed, when a team is "drifting", or when changes require a new vision.

Leaders are the custodians of the vision, which provides focus and reminds everyone of what is really important. These skills are crucial at Level 7 of Barrett's model.

Research suggests that this aspect is very important in motivating people; by continually reminding people of the larger purpose of their work, the visionary leader gives meaning to people's work. People can see they are contributing to something worthwhile, which is an important contributor to employees' engagement.

The visionary leader must have:

- confidence in order to create a vision that rings true; and
- empathy to understand other's perspectives and how they feel so they can align the vision to the values of the people they lead.

	Note to self: To what extent am I using this style and what has been the impact?

Reflection

For each of the six styles and skill sets listed above, reflect on how much of your time is spent on each (as a rough percentage), then indicate what you believe your current skill level is and changes you want to make.

Leadership skills	Percentage of time I spend on this	My current skill level (Unskilled/ Skilled/Very Skilled)	Notes to self: actions I will take
Command			
Affiliative			
Pace-setting			
Participative			
Coach			
Visionary			

Important qualities for leaders

In the Conscious Leader/Full Spectrum Leader approach to leadership, there is a strong focus on the personal qualities of the leader. To be a leader who is trusted, respected, inspiring and able to bring out the best in others, a commitment to ongoing personal development is the starting point.

Leadership greatness rests on our personal greatness; our quality of being determines our quality of doing. We cannot be a better leader than we are as a person – our character is at the core of how we lead. We want to be leaders who are trusted and able to engage and inspire our followers to commit their full energy toward the purpose of the organisation and create value and success. In that case, we need to not only reflect on what we are doing as leaders, but also on how we are showing up as people.

We must be able to manage ourselves before we are able to manage other people as leadership flows from who we are.

The following are important personal qualities we need to be trusted and inspiring leaders:

Passion

Success starts with passion for what you do. Vision also flows from passion. In every article you read about a successful person or business, the words "passion" and "vision" will come up as the starting point.

You may have a passion for your organisation's product or service. I worked in the motor industry for years and many of the people who worked there loved the product and took immense pride in the design and quality of the cars; they would go to extraordinary lengths to build a good quality product. Similarly, I have met people in many other businesses with a great passion for their brand and products. Many leaders have a passion for people and their growth and development. Others love their field of work and have a real passion for activities such as developing business cases on which future strategy is decided, coming up with the most creative marketing campaigns, process improvements on the production line, or ensuring working conditions are safe.

Passion is contagious and energises people to help make it a reality.

Assertiveness

To build a climate of trust and respect, you need to consider your way of relating to the team. When you think about it, in any team you have to balance your needs, concerns and wishes with the needs, concerns and wishes of other people. Let's look at four possible scenarios, leading to four possible styles of behaviour, using the diagram below.

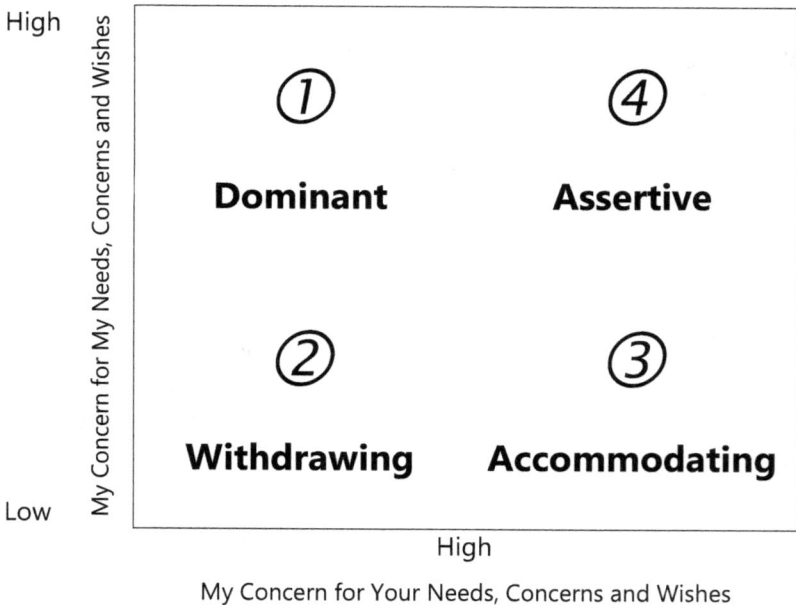

Figure 16: Four possible styles of behaviour

Scenario 1: Here my concern for what I want is high, and my concern for what others want is low. This means that in any situation I will want my own way. This is dominant or aggressive behaviour. When you are in this mode, people around you will perceive you as:

■ forceful; talks a lot;

■ pushing your ideas and not really listening to others;

■ stubborn;

■ unresponsive or insensitive to other people's ideas or feelings;

■ argumentative;

■ arrogant; and

■ self-centred; wanting your own way.

People in this mode tend to value their independence and autonomy, and like to have power and control over others.

If this is your usual style, harmonious relationships will not be the result, and if there are a few people in the team with this style, open warfare will be the norm!

Scenario 2: Here my concern for what I want is low; possibly I have little courage to express my views, or maybe it's just not that important to me. I am also not really concerned about what others want. This is withdrawing behaviour. When you are in this mode, people will perceive you as:

■ passive and uninvolved;

■ backing down easily;

■ tending to avoid issues;

■ taking a back seat;

■ letting things happen;

■ reluctant to express an opinion;

■ uninvolved;

■ unresponsive to the needs or concerns of others;

■ guarded and careful what you say.

People who are in this mode often like security and predictability.

Again, this approach will not build relationships of trust and openness, as people will not know where you stand on any issue.

Scenario 3: Here, as above, my concern for my needs and wishes is still low, but now I am highly concerned about your needs and wishes. This is accommodating behaviour – I am happy if you are happy! In this mode, people will experience you as:

- warm and responsive;
- open and caring;
- sensitive to others and their needs;
- quick to compromise;
- unassertive;
- reluctant to take a stand on issues;
- glossing over difficult issues; and
- friendly and social.

People who adopt this style have strong needs for acceptance and want to be liked at all costs. They often have problems setting clear personal boundaries.

Again, this will not build great relationships in the long-term. If you are in this mode too much, you will soon feel that you are being taken advantage of and your resentment will build up over time. Also, your team members who have more dominant styles will tend to ride roughshod over you. If there are too many people in the team with this style, there will be little debate or challenge and decisions made will not have been thoroughly evaluated. There will be more emphasis on good relationships and not "rocking the boat".

Scenario 4: In this scenario, you have a high concern for the views and wishes of others, but you also have a high concern for your own views, wishes and needs. This is assertive behaviour. In this mode, people will experience you as:

- open and clear about your views;
- responsive to their views;
- willing to engage in open discussion and debate;
- open-minded and flexible;
- showing respect for others' views, needs and feelings;
- a good listener; and
- willing to look for creative solutions everyone can support.

People who are mostly in this mode have strong needs for growth and self-development, and want to make a contribution. They realise that listening to the people around them they will broaden their understanding and that this will lead to better and more creative decisions.

This style will build a great team as you are open about your views and wishes, but also willing to listen and understand the views of others and to make decisions which all can support.

Personal styles: Your area of growth

There are two main skills you need to work on to be in the assertive style:

- Courage to be open and to express your views clearly and constructively.
- Respectful listening to fully understand the views of others.

What this basically means is that there must be a concern for your own benefit and well-being, as well for the benefit and well-being of others in the team. To achieve this balance there needs to be a commitment in the team to keep the channels of communication open and to work through problems.

Time to reflect

What would you say is your dominant style? Where is your area of growth? If your most-used style is in the:

- dominant quadrant, then your area of growth is to consider the needs of others as well as your own. This requires a higher level of skill in Listening and Collaborating;

- withdrawing quadrant, then you need to work on being more open with your views and feelings and to engage more with people to find out what their views and feelings are;

- accommodating quadrant, the issue for you could be to be more assertive and to be clearer about your own boundaries in terms of what you are or are not willing to accept; or

- assertive quadrant, acknowledge these qualities within yourself and keep on honing your skills of listening actively and of being constructively clear and candid.

Recognise that this process of looking for solutions that meet the needs of all is how you and the team will make more creative decisions.

Think of people as your teachers

Every day you have to deal with people in different quadrants and each one will present a particular challenge and a particular growth opportunity for you. Very often we wish other people would change, but this is simply a way of distracting ourselves from our own growth needs. Instead, let's take the view that it is impossible to change another person – only they can do that. Our best strategy is to grow ourselves by developing new strategies and skills to deal with any difficulties our colleagues, customers or managers present us. This approach will reduce the amount of stress and frustration we experience when people do not behave as we think they should.

Self-empowerment

The first step in self-empowerment is to work from our Locus of Control; some things are in our power to control and some are not. For this reason, we need to do a good job of controlling the things we can control and not waste so much energy on the things we cannot. There are things we cannot control, but with some effort we can influence them and then there will be fewer things going wrong that we could have prevented. Then we will have more time to deal with the things we cannot control if they do go wrong.

This requires a proactive approach, where we focus on the issues we can control in order to prevent problems. For example, as a leader, if I focus on improving the work processes, developing employees' skills, clear communication, building people's engagement, systems to measure performance and identifying problems quickly, I will experience fewer problems and crises.

Every work process has inputs and outputs, so if I focus on the inputs and ensure a stable process and well-trained employees, less will go wrong and people will enjoy their work more.

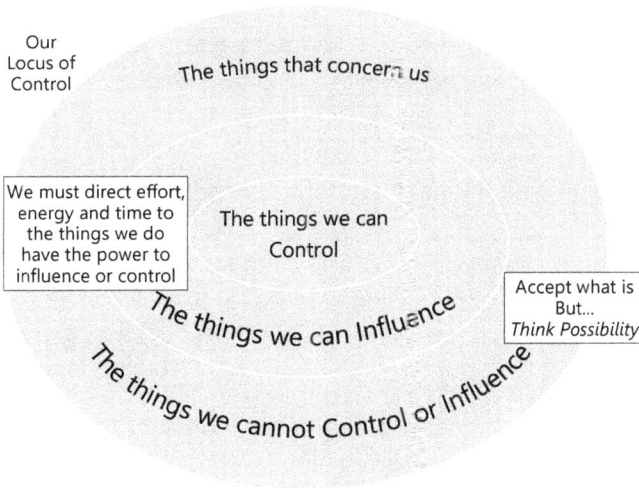

Figure 17: Our Locus of Control

Integrity, authenticity and courage[109]

Individuals with integrity are able to build trusting relationships with others. A culture of integrity is highly valued as it creates an environment of trust and safety. A leader with integrity and high ethical standards conveys a commitment to fairness and a confidence that both they and their employees will honour the rules of the game.

Leaders with integrity live from a place of conviction. Even if external circumstances are chaotic or unclear, a leader with integrity is guided by their values. When you know the "why", the "what" becomes crystal clear. They speak their truth and listen with respect to what is true for others.

As a leader, you have decision-making power. Your team and your management need to trust that you will use it well and:

■ be reliable and responsible;
■ remain true to your word and honour your commitments;
■ stick to the rules of the organisation;
■ exercise caution and take calculated risks; and
■ consistently do the right thing for the organisation.

At times, integrity may require courage to act on your values, but we have to make sure that we walk our talk if we want a reputation of integrity.

To be a person with integrity, authenticity and courage, you need to:

■ be clear on what you stand for. What are your values and beliefs? Thinking and acting with integrity arises when you understand your own values and why you do what you do; and

■ make decisions based on core values. What will be for the greater good or what will lead to the fulfilment of our vision? If you make decisions based on what will make you look good and help your career, people will question your integrity.

An authentic person lives according to their values and speaks their truth. However, this does not mean giving ourselves permission to be dogmatic. An authentic person realises their values and beliefs reflect where they are now, and these may grow as a result of new experiences or influences. They are open to learning from others and from new experiences, and are constantly learning and expanding. Authentic people also consider the impact of their views and behaviour on others and have a regard for others' beliefs and values. They know they have the right to share their views but they do so carefully, realising we are all "work-in-progress".

To be a person of integrity may also mean having to say "No" on occasions, or "Let me think about it and get back to you". If the answer is "No", explain the reasons so people get to know where you stand on issues.

Empathy and compassion

Empathy is an important building block in good relationships. It is the ability to understand another person's feelings about a situation, to see the situation from their perspective, and to understand how they are experiencing it. Empathy requires that we listen without judging; we should understand the importance of the issue for the person and the impact it has on them.

Leaders with empathy can recognise the needs of clients, customers, colleagues and team members, and by using these insights they are better able to build relationships of trust and respect, a positive organisational climate, and high engagement.

Judgement and perspective

Every day as a leader you make decisions, often about complex issues. Your people want to know they can trust your judgement because you take the time to:

- think things through;
- check your assumptions;
- ask for input from others and take a wider view;
- weigh up all the input and consider the situation from all angles; and
- make a decision.

Employees respect a leader with good judgement who can offer a sound perspective on issues.

Confidence and optimism[110]

When we believe in ourselves and our abilities, we are more likely to step forward and take actions in the direction of our vision and values. If we lack self-confidence we will most likely not take positive actions because we don't feel good enough, clever enough or "whatever" enough. This means we will be unlikely to experience the rewards of success or learn the lessons of failure.

When we are confident in our abilities, we will put in the time and effort required and persevere when there are difficulties. When success is achieved, this feeds our confidence, meaning we take on bigger challenges. This leads to an upward spiral of success and well-being. In this way, confidence and optimism or a positive mindset come before success! We need to build our confidence in order to take the steps needed.

> "The difference between people who are thriving and those who are stuck in hopelessness is that they are living in different realities."
>
> **—Sean Achor**

Optimism, i.e. a positive mindset, is often misunderstood. Optimistic and positive people do not ignore or not see problems. Rather they believe success is possible and problems can be overcome. Pessimists tend to think success is not possible. What is the lens through which we view the world?

This does not mean that we become an 'irrational optimist' who thinks magical things will happen without any effort on our part and we can ignore the risks or problems. We need a view on the world that is real and positive. This is what Sean Achor refers to as "Positive Genius"; someone who can see the possibilities as well as the obstacles and risks, but believes that with collective intelligence and effort, we can achieve a good outcome.

To develop confidence and a positive outlook on life we need to tune into our self-talk or the "voice in our head" and check how it is influencing our thoughts about ourselves and our situation. If we mostly hear downward spiral messages such as: it will fail, no-one will listen to you, you are not clever enough and so on, then it is time to find a good coach who can help you reflect and re-wire, as those thoughts are usually not true and will not help you move forward. The role of positive emotions and engagement was confirmed by the "Broaden-and-Build" theory of Fredrickson.[111]

Positive emotions have been found to broaden people's cognitive abilities such as attention and creativity, and build personal resources such as resilience and engagement. The broaden-and-build theory suggests an upward spiral in which positive emotions and broadened thinking lead to increases in emotional and physical well-being, i.e. a state of flourishing. According to Fredrickson, "When positive emotions are in short supply, people get stuck. But when positive emotions are in ample supply, people take off. They become generative, creative, resilient, ripe with possibility and beautifully complex". Positive emotions, confidence and engagement seem to feed each other and lead to great outcomes in terms of success at work and a sense of well-being.

Gratitude, which can be defined as "noticing and appreciating the positive in one's work life", has been found to have an impact on positive emotions. In one study, people were asked to record things they were grateful for in their job at least three times a week for two weeks. They found that this gratitude intervention was associated with a significant increase in positive emotion and engagement.[112]

In another study of the differences between high and low performing teams, it was found that the highest-performing teams had a 5:1 ratio of positive to negative communication, while low performing teams had a 3:1 ratio of negative to positive statements.[113]

Humility

Humility is an important quality for building trust, however it is not well-understood. People tend to confuse humility with a lack of confidence, low status, unassertiveness or poor self-esteem.

The opposite of humility is arrogance or ego-driven behaviour, both of which break down trust.

If a team has the belief that their leader is self-absorbed, opinionated, indifferent to other viewpoints, mainly focused on self-promotion and making decisions that are best for their personal agenda, they will find it difficult to believe that this person will do what is best for them.

No question, we must have confidence in our strengths, our decision-making abilities and in our contribution to the success of our organisations, however humility balances that as it includes an acceptance that:

- we don't have all the answers and we know what we don't know;
- we can learn from others;
- others have contributed to our success; and
- we too have made mistakes and judgement errors.

People with humility make fewer mistakes because they are open to the views of others and are not arrogant enough to believe they are infallible. We tend to learn humility the hard way, i.e. once we have disregarded important input and done it our way and maybe failed, or once we have alienated colleagues or team members by taking all the credit.

Humility is an important quality of the Conscious Leader. One way to show humility and open up the route to a culture where people feel free to contribute their views is by repeatedly telling the team, "I need your input in case I miss something". If we are open, ask for upward feedback and disclose our own mistakes, failures and the insights we have learned from them, it will make it easier for others to do the same, which earns the leader trust and respect.

Adaptability, innovation and creativity

Adaptability means we are open to new ideas, willing to change our views or change our course of action when required, and accept that the approaches of the past may not be the route to future success.

Adaptable or agile leaders are tuned into their environment in order to pick up signals so that they are able to innovate and respond to new opportunities or challenges. We need to make an effort to understand viewpoints that differ from our own and engage with people who are not like us. Further, we must immerse ourselves in new experiences and environments in order to open our minds and see new possibilities.

"I don't think you can solve problems unless you're curious about them, and so much of what we do is solving problems or looking at innovations in our supply chain or working with complicated issues around partnerships or innovations, to me that's a natural quality that you've got to have–about business, your colleagues, challenges– it helps you be a better leader. We need a world full of people asking deep questions or else we're not going to have a world to live in."– Rose Marcario (Patagonia CEO)

Resilience

The pace of change and complexity in the business world has increased dramatically, leading many people to feel overworked and overwhelmed.

When we are resilient, we are able to face challenges calmly and with a clear mind; we develop confidence in our ability to handle any situation life throws at us. Resilience is about responding with inner strength to the demands made on us on a daily basis.

Great leaders are able to bounce back from adversity, so we need to develop qualities and behaviours that will protect us from the potential harmful effects of workplace stress and turmoil, and help us to thrive during difficult circumstances.

Resilient people face their hardships. They make a deliberate choice to do something about their difficult situation, while at the same time checking that their emotions do not become negative. They do not allow themselves to become overwhelmed by their own emotions; they manage to stay positive and optimistic, expecting that things will work out well in the end. They believe that they will be successful and overcome their difficulties.

Resilient people are also very determined; they refuse to accept failure and persevere with their efforts even when they experience some setbacks. They face and deal with the obstacles that come their way and make use of the support of their friends, colleagues and family.

You may wish to explore the HeartMath techniques to deal better with stress and be more resilient.[114]

Mindfulness, self-awareness and self-regulation

Being mindful means being aware of our perceptions, our emotions, the reasons for our actions, and our values and goals. We understand that we take actions based on our understanding of a situation and we ask ourselves how we came to the conclusions and decisions we did, and if we have sound reasoning for these. We need to be aware of what we are thinking, because our thoughts create our emotional state and drive our behaviour. In this way we confront reality and expand our understanding of our outer and inner worlds. We remember what is important to us and make conscious choices in line with our values and vision. We also develop an awareness of others and try to understand their deeper motivations.

When we first take on a leadership role, we tend to be very aware of how we interact with others and the impressions we are making.

Over time, as our confidence increases, we may be less aware of the impact we are having on others. The most effective leaders have a high degree of self-awareness about the emotional states that they are experiencing and expressing, and as a consequence, creating in others around them.

As we can see from the diagram below, between an incident and our response, we have choice. For example, if a team member does not meet an important deadline, I have the choice to:

■ react, maybe expressing anger, frustration and blame; or

■ breathe, calm down, examine my assumptions and choose a response in line with my values, e.g. find out what happened, how the problem can be resolved and then decide how the employee should be handled.

My choice has consequences for my reputation, for the employee and for the team. A disempowered person who reacts will blame other people or the situation for their behaviour (he made me angry), whereas an empowered person will always take responsibility for their behaviour (I reacted without thinking).

We always have a choice. We cannot always choose what happens to us, but we can choose how we deal with what happens to us.

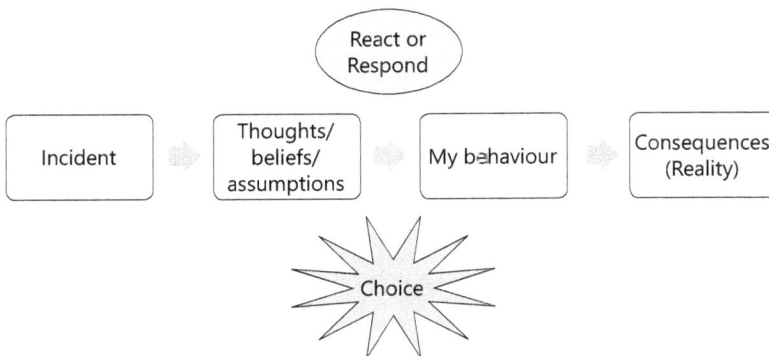

Figure 18: Exercising choice in how we respond to situations

Leaders who are able to regulate their emotions effectively create a stable environment, whereas leaders who are stressed, frustrated or angry can create toxic work environments. People quickly pick up on signals such as tense body language, scowling and eye rolling, however a calm, stable leader will help others to experience similar states. This empowers people to think more clearly, innovate and perform at their best.

Of course we are only human – even the best leaders will have their bad days when they react badly, but with self-reflection and some humility, we will take steps to correct the situation. As leaders we need strategies that keep us calm and stable so that the people around us are not also stressed and anxious.

According to Richard Branson, "In business, know how to be a good leader and always try to bring out the best in people. It's very simple: listen to them, trust in them, believe in them, respect them, and let them have a go!"[115]

Personal reflection on the individual qualities of great leaders
Reflect on the qualities listed above and identify where you are already strong.
Identify one or two qualities you wish to strengthen. List specific actions you will take to strengthen these.

I witnessed the impact of great leadership recently when I was coaching young, top performing employees participating in a talent development programme.

Young people have a bad reputation for "job hopping", but two of the group I was coaching had been in the same jobs for over five years and were both regarded as top performers. This normally meant that they would be mobile.

I asked them about their careers and both said they had considered changing jobs to add to their CV, but both said they did not want to leave their manager.

What they described was a Servant Leader/Conscious Leader approach which was bringing out the best in them. They both spoke about how their managers took a personal interest in them and encouraged them to take on greater responsibilities. They said they were not afraid to take on challenging new roles at work because they knew their managers who "had their backs". Further, their managers tried to match work to their strengths and interests, and were available to them to discuss problem situations and to coach them on how to approach these.

There was plenty of encouragement, praise and public recognition. Both said they were prepared to put in long hours to get the job done and they knew their managers were flexible and trusting if they needed time off.

They also spoke about their managers' calm temperaments and consultative approaches. Team meetings were fun and energetic, and all team members were willing to support each other if there was unusual pressure. One person mentioned that at the end of every day her manager would say, "Good-bye and thank you for everything today", so she always left on a high and looked forward to the next day.

They both felt that if they had made mistakes, it was very easy to go to their managers, tell them about it and have a conversation about how to sort things out quickly. You would only be in trouble if you did not highlight a mistake.

Summary

Summary
☐ —
☐ —
☐ —

Leaders play an enormous role in the engagement of their people. Our role is to set a clear direction, unleash the energy and intelligence of our team, and be committed to their growth.

Yet leadership is messy and complex with no guarantee of success. We will all experience great days as well as terrible days when we doubt ourselves. We have to deal with tough conversations; make hard decisions without always being able to share the context with our team so we hope they trust us; take responsibility when things go wrong; and give others the credit when it goes right.

Knowing we don't always have the answers, having to maintain high positive energy in the team when we don't have it ourselves on some days, having to patiently coach someone when we think its quicker to do it ourselves, listening to people's aspirations and knowing we cannot meet them in the short or medium term, and dealing with internal politics are all part of the job description.

The only way to succeed in the long term is to be clear about your leadership values and the reputation you want as a leader, to accept you will not always live up to it and not be so hard on yourself, to self-reflect, to renew yourself and to resolve to do better tomorrow.

Learning and evolving is essential. Surround yourself with people who will support you, be honest with you and who want you to succeed. Stay focused on where you're going and celebrate your successes as you go.

The rewards of leadership are great; meaningful connections, great results, seeing people grow and develop, and witnessing your own growth and confidence. Then you know you are contributing something unique and amazing to the world and it will all be worth it.

Personal reflection: Your leadership story
Take time to reflect on the information in this chapter, your own leadership journey up until now, and your leadership beliefs that will take you forward.
How has the leadership theme shown up in your life so far?
If you were to give your leadership story a name, like the title of a book or a movie, what would you call your story?
What beliefs or ideas underpin your leadership story? What has been your success formula so far?
Where did these ideas on leadership come from, i.e. what has been the greatest influence on you as a leader? ▪ Who has had a positive impact on your beliefs about leading and motivating people? ▪ What did you learn from these people? ▪ What was the one event that helped you to become the leader you are today?

How have these beliefs influenced the way you see yourself, your work and the people who are important to you?
Where will these beliefs take you? Is that where you want to be heading? Will there be changes to these beliefs?
What do you now believe is important for a leader?
Picture your retirement or farewell party. What do you want people to say about you?
What do you expect of your people?
What can people expect from you in a leadership role?

Rochelle and Nicholas conclude their coaching sessions

"It has been a lot to absorb", said Rochelle. "I'll certainly write up my intentions as a leader. I can see that leadership for high engagement is lifelong work. I'll come back to these notes many times and reflect. Thank you for putting me on this path. I will grow as a person and as a leader, and I hope to be able to look back at the positive role I have played in developing talented people as well as my impact on the company's success."

Section 3

HR's role in supporting employee engagement

The preceding chapters dealt with the individual leader's role in the engagement of his or her team, however leaders do not operate in a vacuum – they are part of a larger system and workplace culture.

In Chapter 7 we will look at how to go about administering an employee engagement survey.

In Chapter 8, Laurisha, the head of HR from Chapter 1, will outline what she believes is a good strategy to address employee engagement.

Chapter 7

Measuring employee engagement

....

> In this chapter, we focus on using Employee Engagement
> surveys, how to use the survey results and examples of
> Employee Engagement questions.

We saw in Chapter 1 how important employee engagement is to any
organisation. It is a key input into business results such as customer
experience, productivity and quality, making it an important focus
area for management and HR. Management often needs HR to help
them connect the dots, however.

If the following business results are not looking good...

- customer experience
- productivity
- quality
- absenteeism
- turnover among your talented employees

...then it is time to reflect on the state of employee engagement in
the company as it may be a contributing factor.

Before employee engagement can be achieved, management and HR
need a number of questions answered:

- What is the current level of employee engagement?
- Does it differ across the company?
- What are the factors influencing employee engagement?
- Do we know what employees appreciate as well as what
  disengages them?
- What can we do to manage those factors?

HR will often recommend that an employee survey be carried out as the first step in managing employee engagement. Many organisations use formal, large-scale surveys to measure how employees feel about their jobs and the workplace. Increasingly, companies are supplementing these by using other forms of engagement data as well, to gain ongoing real-time data regarding employees' views of their experience at work. The most common methods used are more frequent "pulse surveys" and real-time analytics from sources other than formal surveys. This is certainly an emerging area of competence for HR people.

Highly engaged organisations are more likely than less engaged organisations to measure engagement continuously, showing the value of the information from these surveys.

As the HR leaders providing our organisations with engagement surveys, we need to challenge ourselves. Are our engagement surveys really measuring the factors that contribute to engagement and specific drivers of performance? Or do we have a list of questions we think are important and maybe have little relation to real employee engagement issues?

Consider how the workplace has changed over the past 10 years or so... flatter organisational structures; fewer managers with wider spans of control; younger employees, possibly with different value systems and views on work; new technologies; and a workforce made up of full-time employees, contractors and remote workers. The line between work and private time has blurred with smartphones, e-mails and WhatsApp groups. All of this means that we must ask ourselves if we are still measuring what is important to employees in our engagement surveys.

The best-case scenario is that we offer our organisation a survey that asks the questions that need to be asked, and we use the results to develop action plans and strategies that make the company a really awesome place to work.

The worst-case scenario is that we offer the organisation a survey with lots of questions we think are important, but we are not really sure if this survey is measuring the factors that bring out the best in people and make them want to stay. Then we use the results to develop action plans and strategies, using up a lot of people's time and company resources, that have no or little impact on engagement among our employees.

There is a huge market of employee survey providers. Deloitte claims the industry is valued at approximately $1 billion, and is staffed by industrial psychologists who have built statistical models that correlate turnover with various employment variables.[116] Gallup was the pioneer in this field with the Gallup Q12, which consists of 12 questions that predict engagement and retention.[117] Other vendors have developed their own models, which are mainly focused on the characteristics of leadership, management, career opportunities, and other elements of the work environment.

For an employee survey to add value, many issues need to be thought through. Below is a process flow that lists the main issues, which are relevant to an annual company-wide survey as well as to the more frequent "pulse" surveys.

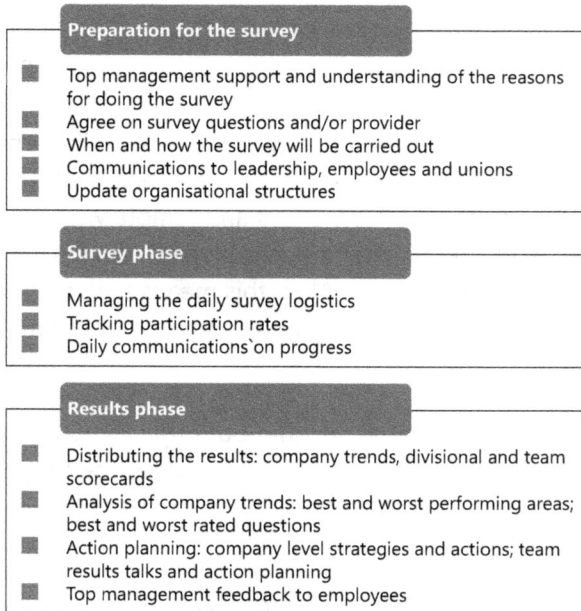

Preparation for the survey

- Top management support and understanding of the reasons for doing the survey
- Agree on survey questions and/or provider
- When and how the survey will be carried out
- Communications to leadership, employees and unions
- Update organisational structures

Survey phase

- Managing the daily survey logistics
- Tracking participation rates
- Daily communications on progress

Results phase

- Distributing the results: company trends, divisional and team scorecards
- Analysis of company trends: best and worst performing areas; best and worst rated questions
- Action planning: company level strategies and actions; team results talks and action planning
- Top management feedback to employees

Figure 19: Process flow listing main issues

The employee engagement survey process

The preparation phase

Top management support and understanding for the employee engagement survey

There needs to be a good understanding of what employee engagement is among top management. What does it mean and how does it support business results? Once that has been achieved, they will want to know more about employee engagement levels in the company and what is affecting them either positively or negatively. Top management also need to understand that a structured survey process will be followed to make sure the results are useful to all levels of management, and that actions must follow to address major employee concerns. These actions will take place at the company, division and team levels.

Agree on survey questions and/or provider

An important consideration is what you will measure in the engagement survey and who will manage the survey process. You can use an external provider with well-validated questions and top-class survey infrastructure, or you can decide to formulate your own survey questions and either run the survey in-house or contract with a company to run the survey for you, using your questions.

Many companies prefer to use companies that specialise in employee engagement, as their survey questions have been rigorously tested, they have the IT infrastructure to manage a hassle-free survey, and they can provide professional scorecards to each manager.

According to Mark Murphy, survey questions usually include the following topics:[118]

- Leader engagement: How employees are connected to and energised by their leaders.

- Job engagement: How involved and absorbed employees are in their work.

- Team engagement: To what degree employees are motivated and energized by their co-workers.

- Organisational engagement: How passionate employees are about the organisation as a whole.

Employees often have concerns about confidentiality and are usually reassured when told the survey is not being run by company employees and that the survey company refuses to share any individual scores, even if the CEO demands to know!

Some of the organisations that specialise in employee engagement surveys include Gallup, Towers Perrin, Deloitte, Best Place to Work, Gartner, Korn Ferry and Hay Group.

The downside is that the costs often seem very high and there is no choice regarding the questions, although some companies do offer the option to add additional company-specific questions to their standard set of questions.

Developing your own company-specific questions may be more difficult than you might think as the questions need to be very clear and unambiguous, and must measure topics that support employee engagement. Achieving buy-in from management for the questions can also be a difficult process as they often want to add in many untested questions.

The next consideration is an IT system that can capture each employee's score, ensure employee confidentiality, and generate meaningful and user-friendly results and scorecards. Developing a system might be a long and costly process, in which case it is often a better option to contract with a survey company to administer the survey for you.

Small companies may look at using tools like SurveyMonkey or Google Chrome.

Examples of employee engagement questions

The **Gallup Q12** is based on extensive research and has been administered to more than 25 million employees in 189 countries. These questions, Gallup says, constitute, "the best predictors of employee and workgroup performance". The first two criteria on the list address employees' primary needs, while the others address three stages: how workers contribute to the whole and are valued, organisational fit, and development:[119]

1. Do you know what is expected of you at work?
2. Do you have the materials and equipment to do your work right?
3. At work, do you have the opportunity to do what you do best every day?
4. In the last seven days, have you received recognition or praise for doing good work?
5. Does your supervisor, or someone at work, seem to care about you as a person?
6. Is there someone at work who encourages your development?
7. At work, do your opinions seem to count?
8. Does the mission/purpose of your company make you feel your job is important?
9. Are your associates (fellow employees) committed to doing quality work?
10. Do you have a best friend at work?
11. In the last six months, has someone at work talked to you about your progress?
12. In the last year, have you had opportunities to learn and grow?

The top nine survey questions from Gartner:[120]

1. Do you understand the strategic goals of the broader organisation?
2. Do you know what you should do to help the company meet its goals and objectives?

3.   Can you see a clear link between your work and the company's goals and objectives?
4.   Are you proud to be a member of your team?
5.   Does your team inspire you to do your best work?
6.   Does your team help you to complete your work?
7.   Do you have the appropriate amount of information to make correct decisions about your work?
8.   Do you have a good understanding of the informal structures and processes at your organisation?
9.   When something unexpected comes up in your work, do you usually know who to ask for help?

As a coach, I use the following statements with clients to establish their "mood" at work and to get a clear picture of what is affecting their engagement.

My job

1.   My job gives me a sense of purpose and contribution, and the opportunity to make a difference.
2.   I have a sense of achievement and success at work.
3.   My job is well-aligned to my strengths and skills.
4.   In my job I use my natural talents.
5.   My job is well-aligned to my personal values; I am doing something I believe is important.
6.   I love the kind of work I do.
7.   I am growing and developing professionally and personally in my job.
8.   My work goals and KPIs are clearly defined; I know what is expected of me at work.
9.   I receive clear and constructive feedback on how well I am doing at work.
10. My input and ideas regarding my goals and KPIs are taken into account.
11. I am satisfied with my work-life balance.
12. I feel that my contribution is recognised and appreciation is shown.
13. I have the authority to make decisions in my job.
14. I am appropriately involved in decisions in my work.

My team

1. I feel proud to be part of this team for their results, impact and contribution.
2. In this team, there is a climate of trust and respect for each other.
3. I have a sense of belonging in this team.
4. Commitment levels are high in this team.
5. In this team there is a culture of innovation and continuous improvement; we are never satisfied with mediocrity.
6. In this team, people are highly skilled and experienced and have what it takes to do the job well.
7. At work I am able to freely raise issues that are important to me, e.g. ideas, problems.
8. At work my ideas and concerns are carefully considered.
9. In this team, we are clear on the team's goals and roles.
10. Our work processes are clear.
11. Communication in this team is good; everyone ensures that team members are well-informed and that we get the information we need when we need it.
12. We have relationships of collaboration, trust and respect with other teams in the organisation.

Leadership

1. I trust my manager/team leader.
2. I feel respected by my manager/team leader.
3. I feel supported by my manager/team leader.
4. My immediate leader is a role model in terms of company values.

Resources/Work environment

1. I have the resources to do what is expected of me.
2. My physical work environment is comfortable and functional.
3. The systems and processes in place are effective and support the achievement of our goals.
4. My work-load is manageable.

The company

1. I am proud to work for...
2. Employee policies and practices are fair to all.
3. I have been treated fairly at this company.
4. I feel secure in my job.
5. I support the vision of the company.
6. I totally support the company values of...
7. Leadership at this company live authentically by the values of the company.
8. The culture and climate in the company brings out the best in people.
9. I feel good about coming to work.
10. I would recommend [company] as a great place to work. (This is the Employee Net Promoter Score and is a way for organisations to measure employee loyalty.)

If you are developing your own survey, one option is to test your questions on a small sample of employees before rolling them out across the organisation.

When and how the survey will be carried out

The timing of the survey is an important topic. You want to choose a time when there is nothing happening that may skew the results, for example a restructuring or merger announcement, a bonus pay out, wage negotiations etc. When management receives the results of the survey and they are either very bad or very good, you do not want them dismissing the results by saying, "Oh yes, it's because of...". Ideally the survey should happen at a time when it's "business as usual".

You also need to decide how much time is necessary to give everyone enough time to participate. This is normally anything from two weeks to a month.

Who is included in the survey?

The other decision is who will participate; is this a company-wide survey or are we targeting specific groups within the company? For example, we may find that we have a high turnover of engineers, so we may want to focus on that specific group.

If it is a company-wide survey, another consideration is if you will exclude anyone. For example, you may have people on overseas assignments who are still part of your organisation. There may be women on maternity leave. There may be employees on suspension for an extended period, or employees who have been off sick for a few months. Will you include new employees with less than three months service? What about contract employees who work side-by-side with the company's employees? Are part-time employees included? If you do exclude any group of people, make sure there is a good rationale for the decision and that the decision is applied consistently.

Accurate organisational structures are essential

Most engagement surveys provide individual managers with a team scorecard. To do this, the company organogram must be up-to-date so that each manager receives feedback from his or her team and not, for example, from people who moved departments some time back. The organogram must then be uploaded onto the survey system. Employees are normally issued with a password which ensures that their answers go into the correct scorecard. To protect confidentiality, teams with less than five people usually do not get a scorecard. The same applies if less than five people in a team take part in the survey.

How to capture each person's responses

Your next challenge in doing the survey is how you will gather each employee's responses. Online is usually the best, but many companies have constraints if there are groups of employees who are not able to work on a computer or if it is difficult for employees to access a computer.

One big manufacturer with a large group of shop floor employees was not able to allow people to leave the moving production line to complete the engagement survey, so they issued each employee with a password letter and a paper copy of the survey. They stopped the production line for 30 minutes and asked these employees to complete the survey on the paper copy, only entering their password for identification. Students then collected the forms and entered their responses onto the survey system. Because only a password was used, no-one could identify whose form was whose, thereby protecting confidentiality.

Is it a good idea to make employee engagement scores part of management's KPIs?

My view is that it is not a good idea; the message to employees should be that it is not compulsory to do the survey, but we would like them to. Once participation becomes part of management's objectives, some managers pressurise people to do the survey. The same with the final engagement score: some employees say they feel they are not able to be honest in their ratings for fear of upsetting their management who obviously want a good outcome.

Communications to leadership, employees and unions

Once you have the go-ahead from top management for the survey and you have worked out how you will go about doing it, it's then time to communicate your plan to the rest of the organisation. This can be a combination of face-to-face briefings supplemented with information via e-mail, on company notice boards or letters with employees' pay slips. The communications must include why we are doing the survey, when it will take place, assurances around confidentiality, what we will be doing with the results and of course, the questions employees will be asked to rate as well as the rating scale. You may decide to give the survey a catchy title such as Pulse or Barometer.

> **True story:** One of the senior managers misunderstood the rating scale: he thought 1 was the top rating. He rated his boss, one of the Directors and a good leader, Poor or Very Poor on all the questions. The Director was distraught, trying to fathom who in his team of senior managers was so unhappy. It was only during the results discussion that this person realised his mistake!

The survey phase

Managing the daily survey logistics

Never underestimate the amount of work required for a successful survey, so be on standby to handle questions and ensure you have a Help Desk to handle queries regarding passwords and access to the system. People lose their passwords, forget their PIN numbers, cannot access the system, are not sure how to rate, and so on.

Tracking participation rates

Most online systems will give you a daily participation rate for the company, divisions and teams, and it is good to keep people informed of the progress as it does help to get people to do the survey. My suggestion is to use fun communications to motivate people to do the survey.

Results and action phase

Distributing the results: Company trends, divisional and team scorecards

Once we have selected and validated our survey questions and run the survey, the key question is what to do with the results once we have them. Is it clear what actions you need to take to address low-scoring items and to maintain the high-scoring items?

Firstly, communicate to all employees once the results are available, with detailed information on how to access their scorecard. Most scorecards are easy to interpret, but it may be a good idea to include a short description of the key information on the scorecard.

Analysis of company trends

It is now time for the analytical work: results need to be interpreted and trends identified. These might include:

- the best and worst performing areas in the company;

- the best and worst rated questions;

- any significant changes compared to previous surveys;

- any significant differences between the various divisions in the company;

- what the company is doing well in terms of employee engagement; and

- the "hot topics" to be addressed.

This information needs to be shared with top management who need to agree on a way forward. Top management usually have a lot of questions about the employee engagement survey results; why is there such a difference between divisions? What are the top-scoring areas doing better than the rest? What is going on in the poorer-scoring areas?

It might be good for HR to explore a little deeper before sharing the results. Focus group sessions always yield good information, so it would probably be wise to talk to a sample of employees from the best and worst scoring areas and ask some open-ended questions, such as:

- What may have affected the results of your division's engagement scores?

- What has been the biggest positive impact on your engagement at work? What makes you like your job?

- What are the biggest frustrations at work? What makes you dislike your job?

- What are your recommendations to top management regarding making this company a great place to work?

When you as HR report on the survey results to top management, you now have some context to the results.

Gallup's recommendation is that you give special attention to those employees who are high performers, highly engaged and have extensive experience in the organisation, as they understand your business, your customers and what can and cannot be changed. In this way you are more likely to create a workplace that attracts more people like your top employees. By asking for the opinions of your top performers and taking action on their recommendations, you will help create a better organisation where talented people want to work and grow.[121]

Do not 'name and shame' the leaders with poor engagement scores: things are not always as they seem...

I came across a scorecard with a very low engagement score of around 40%. The scorecard was awash with red, i.e. Strongly Disagree. Fortunately, the leader in question agreed to me holding a workshop with the team concerned as he was devastated. I started asking for feedback from the team who soon informed me they were very engaged and loved their jobs; they also thought their eader was great. However, the artisan group received a lower salary increase than the shop floor operators which they felt was unfair, and they used the employee survey to highlight their dissatisfaction. They were shocked when I commented that a score like this could have raised serious doubts in the minds of top management about their leader's ability to lead.

Another very poor scorecard was highlighted in a similar situation; a possible outsourcing for part of the team had been raised a few weeks before the survey and people were upset and insecure and rated most of the questions Strongly Disagree as a way of venting, even though they thought highly of their leader.

So these isolated incidents do happen; we need to first explore the reasons before concluding we have a leadership problem.

Results talks and action planning: Company-level strategies and actions.

Once top management have the results of the survey, they are responsible for identifying and addressing company-wide engagement initiatives. This is when they often turn to HR for guidance.

HR may be tasked to develop strategies to address the problem areas highlighted in the survey. Examples of company-wide initiatives as a result of the engagement survey might include:

- the CEO addressing the workforce every quarter on company strategy, plans and performance;

- a review of the talent management process to ensure people with good potential for leadership are being identified and developed;

- the topic of employee engagement principles being included in the company's leadership development programme;

- the IT division being tasked to assist leadership to automate outdated manual systems;

- cross-divisional workshops being held to strengthen collaboration and break down silos;

- a company-wide recognition scheme being introduced;

- the policy on part-time studies being reviewed and updated so that employees can more easily enhance their qualifications;

- team or individual coaching being offered to leaders who request this;

- a fresh initiative being launched to strengthen the company values and culture; and

- the onboarding process for new employees being refreshed and updated.

Buy-in and support from top leadership is essential, so careful research needs to be undertaken to ensure the relevance and effectiveness of the proposed initiatives, as well as excellent implementation.

Results talks and action planning

Now that individual leaders have information on their employees' perceptions and feelings, they are usually totally confused! HR support is therefore needed to guide them through this process. Managers are responsible for addressing their team's engagement issues. The team results talk is very important as when leaders send out an employee survey but take no action on the results, it can lead to lower engagement than doing no survey at all.

Senior managers need to take ownership of the outcomes of the leaders reporting to them by reviewing their scorecards with them, providing coaching and offering any other support required, such as leadership development, mentoring or any other internal support.

A set of guidelines like the ones below will help leaders through the process.

The first step leaders must take is to ensure their team members see the scorecard.

Secondly, each leader needs to analyse the scorecard and identify the following:

- How many people participated in the survey? What does that tell me? How do I interpret a high or a low participation rate?

- What is the overall engagement score? Is it better or worse than previous surveys? How does it compare to the overall company or divisional score? Should I be happy with this score or should I be concerned? Were there any special circumstances during the past year that may have influenced the results?

- What are the top three and the bottom three scores? What is my understanding of the reasons for this? What may have contributed to these results?

- If this is a regular annual survey, reflect on the actions we took after the last survey. Can I see the impact of these in this year's results? What worked well and what did not work so well in terms of engagement?

Thirdly, good leaders listen and understand before they take action, so each leader must set up a special "results talk" session with the team. Now if the scorecard is good, it's an easy conversation: the team explains the reasons for the good scores and makes a few suggestions to remove some small frustrations. The manager is happy.

If the scorecard is poor, however, it's a terrible meeting; no-one wants to talk about anything and no-one remembers scoring any item low. If a team member is not at the meeting, the team may conclude he or she gave the low rating!

This is where HR plays an important support role by providing skilled facilitators for these discussions. One option is to have the manager present with the facilitator leading the discussion, while another option is for the facilitator to meet the team without the manager and to then give them feedback after the session.

It is always good to follow an appreciative enquiry approach at these sessions: focus on what is working as well as how things could be better.

It's complicated! The results talks are important as scorecards do not tell the full story. Recently I worked with a team where the question on the company value of 'Integrity' had equal ratings in the categories of Strongly Agree, Agree, Disagree and Strongly Disagree. The leader was very worried, so I asked the team to define Integrity and to then explain the ratings:

Person 1 rated Strongly Agree and said integrity means sticking to agreed processes. He mentioned an incident where he was being pressured by another department to skip some steps in the sign-off of a new system and his manager had supported him by insisting the process be followed.

Person 2 rated Strongly Disagree and said Integrity means fairness. She mentioned an example of an employee who had the opportunity to take part in a special development programme and she felt it had been handled unfairly.

Person 3 also rated Strongly Disagree and said Integrity means transparency. She mentioned rumours that were denied and then later turned out to be true.

This discussion gave the leader a good insight into the issues that affected the ratings, as well as the impact of leadership behaviours on the team.

Here is a suggested approach a leader can follow in his or her own results talk:

Suggested agenda for a team results talk

Make sure you as the leader ask open questions to explore the issues highlighted in the scorecard and listen well.

- Welcome everyone.
- Review the purpose of the meeting:
  - Review our scorecard.
  - Identify what is working well and what we need to address to make work more fulfilling for us all.
  - Agree on two to three action plans.
- Display the scorecard and highlight key trends and information: participation rate, engagement index best and worst scoring items, and any significant changes since the last survey.
- Ask the team to share their overall impressions of the results: what stands out for you? Which question is of most concern to you?
- Focus on the top scoring items: ask the team what contributed to the good score, i.e. what is working well so we know to maintain that?
- Focus on the items of top concern: what contributed to the low scores and what do we need to do about it?
- Agree an action plan with the team. The action plan should consist of:
  - a description of the current situation;
  - a description of the desired situation, i.e. what will success look like?
  - the action steps required to move from the current to the desired situation; and
  - who is responsible for each action step. Try to share the workload among the team as it is important that team members also feel responsible for contributing to high engagement.

- Agree on how you will review progress; one suggestion is that the engagement action plans are reviewed as part of your weekly/ monthly team meetings. Once the action plans are completed, you can ask the team what else you can all do to make this a great place to work. In this way, the focus on engagement and shared responsibility for engagement is maintained on an ongoing basis.

- Remember to give recognition as progress is made.

If the team is not talking openly, or if one or two people dominate, then do this exercise:

- Split the team into pairs and ask them to write on Post-it notes:

    - what is helping me to be engaged at work and do a good job; and

    - requests or suggestions to make this a really great place to work.

- Ask each pair to put up their Post-it notes on a wall or on a flip chart.

- Cluster the Post-it notes into similar themes.

- Work through the items: ask the pair who put up the item to explain more fully what they meant by it. As the leader, listen and ask questions to clarify.

- Thank the team for their feedback. Make the point that we must ensure we continue to do the things that are already working and not neglect these.

- Ask the team to identify the high priority issues from the requests and suggestions list. The team can vote or discuss until they reach consensus.

Maintain the momentum between surveys

Imagine standing on the scale and you note that you are 5 kgs overweight. Then, without doing anything different, you stand on the scale a week later and you are upset because you are still 5 kgs overweight. This is how some companies approach engagement surveys: we run them annually, we look at the results, it is business as usual, and then in a year's time everyone is frustrated because there is no improvement. There are also managers who think once the results talk is over, they can tick off employee engagement as completed!

As HR leaders, we need to maintain a focus on employee engagement activities. For example, regular communication to employees about progress on the company-wide initiatives, as well as quarterly or half-year follow ups with senior managers to review progress on engagement action plans in their divisions. The message needs to be clear that employee engagement is part of the leadership role. HR can also offer shorter pulse-type surveys to see if there is any improvement in the poorer scoring teams, as well as facilitated team workshops where the team can work on team climate and improve work processes.

If employees have the perception that nothing has happened despite their participation in the survey, they start to question if it adds any value and participation rates go down.

New directions in employee engagement surveys

Listening to the voice of employees is an important part of an HR strategy.

Some companies feel that feedback gathered from traditional engagement surveys every year is not frequent enough to provide a complete and current perspective. Many companies now complement their main engagement survey with pulse surveys or short topic-specific surveys, which help them to react faster to the insights gained.

The main problem with this approach is survey "fatigue"; people generally do not want to be bothered with too many surveys asking the same questions. It is also difficult to manage the results talk and action planning process if the surveys are coming around too fast. As a way to deal with the challenge of survey fatigue, an option is to run engagement surveys on a monthly basis but with different groups of employees. In this way each employee is only asked to do the survey once per year, but the organisation is able to keep its finger on the pulse.

If we use a pulse-type survey is for a smaller sample or sub-set of employees, we also need to be careful about how we react to a sudden downward or upward trend which may be temporary and specific to that group only. In these instances, the results talks become very important to explore underlying issues.

HR can use other approaches to "listening" to employees that will help them understand employee experience and help them be able to predict retention, performance and engagement. New technologies make employee analytics a lot easier. Companies are now starting to track trends from many sources, such as:

- attendance;
- sick leave;
- length of service;
- training and development received;
- performance ratings;
- job changes within the company;
- information from exit interviews as well as stay interviews;
- focus groups;
- social analytics on data from platforms such as Glassdoor, LinkedIn, Facebook or Twitter;
- the company recognition programme; and
- innovation management.

For the time being, the annual employee survey is still the norm in companies that do surveys, but a new wave of technology is opening up many other options. New pulse-type survey tools are flooding the market. SurveyMonkey is well known, but look on Google and you will see apps such as:

- SurveyPlanet;
- LimeSurvey;
- QuickTapSurvey;
- YesInsights;
- Survey Anyplace;

- SmartSurvey; and
- Client Heartbeat.

However, even if it is a quick pulse-type survey, the same considerations apply: ask the right questions, produce useful scorecards and do something about the outcomes.

Views against employee engagement surveys

Not everyone is a fan of engagement surveys. Some criticisms are listed below:

- If your employer or leader wants to know how you feel about your job, they shouldn't give you surveys to fill out, they should just ask you!

- Employee engagement surveys are the worst way to take the pulse of your organisation. People believe that if they criticise the boss in their survey feedback, they will feel the repercussions for that offence. What will really happen if the whole team told the truth about a poor leader?

- Surveys are point-in-time exercises. Things keep changing so any snapshot of how people are feeling will have very limited value.

- People try to generalise their comments in order to avoid being identified as the feedback-provider, so their input can become meaningless.

- If a company has to promise confidentiality to get its employees to complete a survey, then you already know you have a lack of trust.

- These surveys are costly to administer and take significant manager time to follow up.

- Surveys produce quantitative ("what" employees think) but not qualitative results ("why" employees think as they do).

All of these are fair comments and mainly point to good leadership and trust. In a perfect working world with only great leaders, we may not need a survey to know how people feel about work.

Currently the annual/biannual survey is a robust tool for measuring employee engagement. The employee survey does allow for year-over-year comparison and can help identify the causes of highs and lows in engagement. We do need to work around these objections raised, however, mainly by educating the leadership on how to work with the process.

Measuring employee engagement provides HR and leadership in the company a clear picture of how people feel about working at the organisation, and gives guidance on the actions required to improve the company's culture and peoples' experiences at work.

Employee feedback collected through engagement surveys will help HR teams and line leaders to understand more fully what the talent they employ expects and values. It also flags problem areas before they get out of control and helps you see what is engaging people to put in discretionary effort and want to stay at your company.

Collecting employee feedback, listening to your people, sharing with them what you've learned and how the results will be addressed are all important parts of what it means to be a great employer.

Chapter 8

The engagement strategy

Laurisha from HR writes to Daniel the CEO

Laurisha felt weary as she put the phone down after Daniel's ranting. Maybe she should have stayed at her previous company where the people and leadership practices were far more advanced. Laurisha had a good insight into the mood at Rozzby as people confided in her. Maybe it was time for her to move to another company and this time she would be far more careful to find out more about the company culture and not be blinded by the salary.

That night she did not sleep well and found herself wide awake at 3 am. A moment of clarity emerged and Laurisha decided to write to Daniel and give him the strategy from HR that he requested. If he takes offence, too bad, I will get another job. Fired up with coffee and 3 am courage, Laurisha wrote an e-mail to Daniel:

Dear Daniel, thank you for your call this afternoon. You are right, we do have an employee engagement problem. I see it also in the absenteeism figures and in the many disciplinary cases.

However, the employee problems we are seeing I believe is the tip of the iceberg and as the leaders at Rozzby, I think it is time for some reflection.

Rozzby culture

We make parts for vacuum cleaners that no one ever sees, except the vacuum cleaner service agents, and I know you have said many times that it is not possible to inspire people with our product range. It is much easier when you make beautiful clothes, furniture, buildings or cars, or come up with brilliant IT products.

However, we have to ask ourselves, what have we done to create any kind of pride in Rozzby among our employees? I am sure most employees have no idea who our customers are and what they do with our products. Our parts go into the biggest and best quality vacuum cleaners in the world, but we never talk to our employees about this. What is stopping us from putting up a beautiful display on the production line of all the products using our parts? We could put up a slogan like "Rozzby; we are part of their success" (pun intended).

Our method of "motivation" at Rozzby is to chase daily production targets and drive down costs. I know that is important, but it cannot be our only method of motivation. We are lacking in heart and soul as a company; daily targets and cost cutting is not inspiring to anyone.

The production managers are extremely stressed because they know you are tracking their performance minute by minute on that big screen in your office. The minute the line stops, all hell breaks loose on the shop floor and there is shouting and swearing until the line starts again.

We installed a system for the workers to stop the line in case of a quality problem, but no one uses it because they are too scared. The quality problems are thus only being picked up at the end of the line, parts are being scrapped, and there is no root cause analysis or training of employees to prevent further problems.

There is a fear culture at Rozzby, which means people do not want to admit to mistakes or take ownership of any problems, hence we have the blaming and avoidance of accountability that goes on. We need to re-look the culture and climate throughout the company.

Another point is that our shop floor workers live in an impoverished community. It was a Rozzby strategy to be close to a poor community so we could pay low wages and rather pay engineers and management top pay rates. Social problems are huge and because of our low wage policy, our workers' lives have not improved and nor has the community benefitted. Our workers believe their lives will never improve working for Rozzby and if the company is successful, only the management and skilled staff benefit. All they see are nicer and newer cars in the management parking bays. There is no real incentive for them to help make the company successful. Their only goal is to just keep their job and they believe that working at the minimum standard, just enough not to get fired, is enough.

If we look beyond the shop floor, our technical experts have no vision beyond keeping the line running. There was a time when our engineers worked closely with our customers to develop innovative solutions and to help make their products better. Our contact with our customers has decreased substantially and our highly skilled engineers are doing routine operational work. Technology enhancements and product development activities are now seen as low priority and will ultimately affect our competitiveness as a supplier. The engineers can see this and are heading to more innovative companies.

My recommendations to improve employee engagement are as follows:

Rozzby's vision and values

What will make all employees proud to work at Rozzby?

- Who are we and what do we stand for? What is our WHY beyond making vacuum cleaner parts? Are we a trusted supplier? A technological innovator? Environmentally responsible? What reputation do we want as a supplier?

- What impact do we want to make on our employees' lives? What reputation do we want as an employer? How will working at Rozzby improve employees' lives?

- What impact do we want to make in the local community? Is there a particular social issue that concerns us? If so, are there NGOs working in that field that we can support? Or maybe we can arrange for our employees to get involved in supporting sports clubs or tutoring pupils etc?

- We need to say what the values are that inspire us as a company and how we should live these out. If we say quality is an important value, then what are the behaviours we want from our leaders and our employees? For example, we want everyone to know why their work is important and to take pride in what they do; we want people to have the necessary skills; we want everyone to be able to do root-cause analysis and learn from mistakes, and so on. And if we say respect is important, will we tolerate leaders swearing at employees?

- Our vision and values should inspire all of us to be better every day and hold ourselves accountable to higher standards of conduct and performance.

- We need a new culture on the shop floor; we need to set up better shop floor management processes where production, quality and engineering work together to find solutions to production problems instead of tossing the problem to the other department.

- Part of our shop floor management must also include ways to communicate production progress and problems to our operators so we can get their input and help to solve these.

Leadership

Once we have defined what we want to be as a company, we need to define what we expect of our leaders. At Rozzby, we promote people into leadership roles who are good technical people and individual achievers, but poor at leading and inspiring people.

210

- We need a clear statement regarding our leadership brand: what can people expect from a Rozzby leader? This must be supported by a competency profile listing the knowledge and skills our leaders must acquire.

- We must assess people applying for leadership roles to ensure they have the potential to meet our leadership standards.

- We need leaders who can bring out the best in people, not people who threaten their people as way to get them to do better work.

Learning and development

- We must provide ongoing leadership development activities that give our leaders the skills they need and opportunities to reflect on how they are leading their people.

  □ Leaders need to know how to bring out the best in people; they need to learn more about how to work with people's strengths, give people a sense of purpose, and coach, develop and communicate in a way that builds trust.

  □ We must consider offering our senior management team the opportunity to work with a coach of their choice so that they become better leadership role models.

- We need training programmes to upskill all employees in their technical roles as well as in skills such as problem solving, interpersonal skills, computer skills, financial skills and so on, depending on their role.

- We must look at ways to upskill our workers so they can take on more responsible and better paying roles in the company, e.g. we can upskill a few operators every year to take up maintenance roles or quality auditor roles.

- We can develop a combination of learning approaches such as trainers on the line, off-site workshops for leaders, e-learning, self-study guides, sponsoring part-time study, benchmarking trips etc.

■ Any learning activities must be followed by application assignments at work so everyone gets the full benefit of the development.

Recruitment

■ If we have a clear vision and values, it will help with recruitment as we can enhance our processes to identify people who want to be part of what we stand for and who have the right skills to make it happen.

Pay and benefits

I know money does not mean you love your job or your boss or your company; you may be here only because you love the money. Pay and benefits can be a big demotivator if people feel underpaid, however, so we need to pay people enough so it's not an issue.

■ We need to benchmark our salaries and wages against national norms.

■ We can investigate performance bonuses for the shop floor if quality and production targets are met consistently.

■ The office environment is looking great and people love the coffee machines, but we need to think about facilities on the shop floor where people can have a lunch break in a comfortable environment. We designed the shop floor for the machines and forgot about the people.

■ We are far from where most of the office staff live so we need to consider some flexibility in terms of start and finish times so people can get a chance to attend to their private affairs. I know it's harder for the shop floor but we need to help out there too where we can.

■ As a company we need to consider our employees' well-being and reduce stress and excessive overtime, and focus on creating a more positive work environment rather than a fear culture.

Recognition

■ People thrive when they feel appreciated and I think we can develop a recognition scheme for teams and individuals who achieve great results or who make an extraordinary contribution or achievement at work.

■ We can include quality awards and process improvement awards, for example for people who have improved their qualifications or done community work; we can customise the scheme to work for us.

■ Maybe for each person or team who wins an award, there can be a donation to a local charity of their choice.

Communication

■ We need to review the information employees get about the company and its achievements, as well as what the different departments are doing. We also need to agree on how we can improve the information sharing within the company. Currently I think people only hear what has gone wrong, they do not hear about successes.

Change management

I believe the top management team must take ownership of the company culture, with the support of HR. I do not believe in a big high impact launch where we promise everyone everything will be different. I believe we must start by defining our vision and values and start to live it at top management level first. We must start with these interventions and programmes I have listed and over time, Rozzby will be a different company to work for.

At some point we should consider an employee engagement survey to get a feel for how our employees feel about their experience of working at Rozzby.

This seems a lot and I might sound very critical, but I have worked in companies where these activities were normal practice and I have seen the positive impact.

I recommend that the top team meet for a day or two off-site with a skilled facilitator to reflect on what kind of a company we wish to be and how we can get started.

As your head of HR, I believe my team has an important role to play and I am willing to support top management to embark on a culture change process to make Rozzby a great company and a great employer.

Kind regards,
Laurisha

What Daniel did

The next morning Laurisha wondered if she had done the right thing. Maybe she should have thought about it more before hitting the 'Send' button.

By late afternoon there had been no word from Daniel about her e-mail and in a management meeting earlier, he seemed very tense and avoided eye contact with her.

At 5 pm a mail from Daniel came through: Hi Laurisha, I read your mail; if it's convenient, please come to my office.

As Laurisha walked into Daniel's office, she saw her mail printed out on his desk with lots of notes in the margin. Daniel leaned back and said, "I didn't really like what I read, but you are right, we have lost our way as a company. We have work to do. How do we start?"

Endnotes

Chapter 1 Endnotes

1   Gallup. 2013. *State of the American Workplace Report: Employee Engagement Insights for U.S. Business Leaders*. Washington, D.C.: Gallup, Inc.
2   Raymundo, O. 2014. *Richard Branson: Companies Should Put Employees First*. Retrieved from: https://www.inc.com/oscar-raymundo/richard-branson-companies-should-put-employees-first.html
3   HR Research Institute. 2018. *The State of Employee Engagement in 2018: Leverage leadership and culture to maximize engagement*. Retrieved from: https://www.hr.com/en/resources/free_research_white_papers/the-state-of-employee-engagement-in-2018-mar2018_jeqfvgoq.html
4   Korn Ferry Institute. 2019. *An Employee Engagement Shutdown*. Retrieved from: https://www.kornferry.com/institute/employee-engagement-shutdown
5   Bersin, J. 2015. *Becoming irresistible: A new model for employee engagement*. Retrieved from: https://www2.deloitte.com/insights/us/en/deloitte-review/issue-16/employee-engagement-strategies.html
6   Bakker, A.B., Demerouti, E. & Xanthopoulou, D. 2012. How do Engaged Employees Stay Engaged? Special Issue. *Ciencia Trabajo*, 14, 15-21.
7   Sorenson, S. 2013. *How Employee Engagement Drives Growth*. Retrieved from: https://www.gallup.com/workplace/236927/employee-engagement-drives-growth.aspx
8   Gallup. 2013. *State of the American Workplace Report: Employee Engagement Insights for U.S. Business Leaders*. Washington, D.C.: Gallup, Inc.
9   Edmans, A. 2016. *28 Years of Stock Market Data Shows a Link Between Employee Satisfaction and Long-Term Value*. Retrieved from: https://hbr.org/2016/03/28-years-of-stock-market-data-shows-a-link-between-employee-satisfaction-and-long-term-value
10 Seligman, M.E.P., Parks, A.C. & Steen, T. 2004. A Balanced Psychology and a Full Life. *The Royal Society*, 359, 1379-1381.
11 Harter, J.K., Schmidt, F.L. & Keyes, C.L.M. 2002. Well-Being in the Workplace and its Relationship to Business Outcomes: A Review of the Gallup Studies. In Keyes, C.L. & Haidt, K. (eds.). *Flourishing: The positive person and the good life*. Washington D.C. American Psychological Association, 205-224.
12 Sinek, S. 2014. *Leaders Eat Last: Why Some Teams Pull Together and Others Don't*. New York: Penguin Group.
13 Lyubomirsky, S. 2008. *The How of Happiness: A New Approach to Getting the Life You Want*. New York: Penguin Books, p26.
14 Gallup. 2013. *State of the American Workplace Report: Employee*

Engagement Insights for U.S. Business Leaders, p3. Washington, D.C.: Gallup, Inc.

15   Ibid.

16   The Conference Board. n.d. *The Engagement Institute: How organizations create and sustain highly engaging cultures*. Retrieved from: https://www.conference-board.org/subsites/index.cfm?id=15136

17   HR Research Institute. 2018. *The State of Employee Engagement in 2018: Leverage leadership and culture to maximize engagement*. Retrieved from: https://www.hr.com/en/resources/free_research_white_papers/the-state-of-employee-engagement-in-2018-mar2018_jeqfvgoq.html

18   Bersin, J. 2015. *Becoming irresistible: A new model for employee engagement*. Retrieved from: https://www2.deloitte.com/insights/us/en/deloitte-review/issue-16/employee-engagement-strategies.html

19   Bakker, A.B. 2011. An Evidence-Based Model of Work Engagement. Current Directions in *Psychological Science*, 20(4), 265-269.

20   Schaufeli, W.B., Bakker, A.B. & Salanova, M. 2006. The Measurement of Work Engagement with a Short Questionnaire. A Cross Cultural Study. *Educational and Psychological Measurement*, 66(4), 701-716.

Chapter 2 Endnotes

21   Re:Work. n.d. *Google's Guide: Understand team effectiveness*. Retrieved from: https://rework.withgoogle.com/print/guides/5721312655835136/

22   Havard Business Review. 2019. *Creating Psychological Safety in the Workplace*. Retrieved from: https://hbr.org/ideacast/2019/01/creating-psychological-safety-in-the-workplace

23   Delizonna, L. 2017. *High-Performing Teams Need Psychological Safety. Here's How to Create It*. Retrieved from: https://hbr.org/2017/08/high-performing-teams-need-psychological-safety-heres-how-to-create-it

24   Sinek, S. 2014. *Leaders Eat Last: Why Some Teams Pull Together and Others Don't*. New York: Penguin Group.

25   Rock, D. 2009. *Your Brain at Work: Strategies for Overcoming Distraction, Regaining Focus, and Working Smarter All Day Long*. New York: Harper Collins.

26   Bruch, H. & Voge, B. 2011. *Fully Charged: How Great Leaders Boost Their Organization's Energy and Ignite High Performance*. Boston, MA: Harvard Business Review Press.

27   Voge, B. 2011. *Manage Your Organization's Energy*. Retrieved from: https://hbr.org/2011/02/manage-your-organizations-ener

28   Brown, B. 2012. *Daring Greatly: How the Courage to Be Vulnerable Transforms the Way We Live, Love, Parent, and Lead*. New York: Penguin Group.

29   Zak, J. 2017. *The Neuroscience of Trust*. Retrieved from: https://hbr.org/2017/01/the-neuroscience-of-trust

30 Business Central. 2019. *7 Simon Sinek Quotes That Will Change Your Thinking on Leadership and Business*. Retrieved from: https://www.businesscentral.net/7-simon-sinek-quotes-that-will-change-your-thinking-on-leadership-and-business

31 Covey, S. 1989. *The 7 Habits of Highly Effective People*. New York: Simon and Schuster, p188.

32 Dutton, J. 2003. *Fostering High-Quality Connections: How to deal with corrosive relationships at work*. San Francisco, CA: Jossey-Bass.

33 Kline, N. 1999. *Time to Think: Listening to Ignite the Human Mind*. London: Cassell Illustrated.

34 Glaser, J. 2013. *Conversational Intelligence: How Great Leaders Build Trust and Get Extraordinary Results*. New York: Bibliomotion, Inc.

35 Ibid.

36 Glaser, J.E. 2014. *Minimize Fear – Maximize Trust: Elevating Conversational Intelligence Elevates Mutual Success*. Retrieved from: https://www.psychologytoday.com/us/blog/conversational-intelligence/201412/minimize-fear-maximize-trust

37 Zak, J. 2017. *The Neuroscience of Trust*. Retrieved from: https://hbr.org/2017/01/the-neuroscience-of-trust

38 Glaser, J. 2013. *Conversational Intelligence: How Great Leaders Build Trust and Get Extraordinary Results*. New York: Bibliomotion, Inc.

39 Cameron, K. & McNaughtan, J. 2014. Positive Organisational Change. *Journal of Applied Behavioural Science*. 50(4), 445-462.

40 Deloitte. 2018. *2018 Deloitte Millennial Survey*. Retrieved from: https://www2.deloitte.com/content/dam/Deloitte/global/Documents/About-Deloitte/gx-2018-millennial-survey-report.pdf

41 Ridgway, R. 2018. *People management: how to create a psychologically safe environment at work*. Retrieved from: https://www.hrzone.com/lead/culture/people-management-how-to-create-a-psychologically-safe-environment-at-work

42 Havard Business Review. 2019. *Creating Psychological Safety in the Workplace*. Retrieved from: https://hbr.org/ideacast/2019/01/creating-psychological-safety-in-the-workplace

43 Delizonna, L. 2017. *High-Performing Teams Need Psychological Safety. Here's How to Create It*. Retrieved from: https://hbr.org/2017/08/high-performing-teams-need-psychological-safety-heres-how-to-create-it

44 Deloitte. 2018. *2018 Deloitte Millennial Survey*. Retrieved from: https://www2.deloitte.com/content/dam/Deloitte/global/Documents/About-Deloitte/gx-2018-millennial-survey-report.pdf

45 Giles, S. 2016. *The Most Important Leadership Competencies, According to Leaders Around the World*. Retrieved from: https://www.speakcdn.

com/assets/1145/the_most_important_leadership_competencies_
according_to_leaders_around_the_world.pdf

46   Liu, A. 2019. *Making Joy a Priority at Work*. Retrieved from: https://hbr.
org/2019/07/making-joy-a-priority-at-work

47   Shawn, A. 2013. *Before Happiness*. New York: Crown Business, p15.

48   Schawbel, D. 2014. *Richard Branson's Three Most Important
Leadership Principles*. Retrieved from: https://www.forbes.com/sites/
danschawbel/2014/09/23/richard-branson-his-3-most-important-
leadership-principles/#16733f593d50

Chapter 3 Endnotes

49   Buckingham, M. & Clifton, D.O. 2005. *Now, Discover Your Strengths*.
London: Pocket Books.

50   Crabb, S. 2011. The Use of Coaching Principles to Foster Employee
Engagement. *The Coaching Psychologist*, 7(1), 27-34.

51   Seligman, M. 2012. *Flourish, A Visionary New Understanding of
Happiness and Well-being*. New York: Simon & Schuster Atria Books.

52   Wesson, K. & Boniwell, I. 2007. Flow Theory-Its Application to Coaching
Psychology. *International Coaching Psychology Review*, 2(1), 33-43.

53   Salanova, S., Llorens, S. & Schaufeli, W.B. 2011. "Yes, I Can, I Feel Good,
and I Just Do It!" On Gain Cycles and Spirals of Efficacy Beliefs, Affect
and Engagement. *Applied Psychology: An International Review*, 60(2),
255-285.

54   Salanova, M., Bakker, A.B. & Llorens, S. 2006. Flow at Work: Evidence for
an Upward Spiral of Personal and Organisational Resources. *Journal of
Happiness Studies*, 7(1), 1-22.

55   Dick, R. 1998. *Setting Your Genius Free*. New York: Berkley Books.

56   Ibid.

57   CliftonStrengths. 2019. *Live Your Best Life Using CliftonStrengths*.
Retrieved from: https://www.gallupstrengthscenter.com/

58   VIA Institute on Character. n.d. *Bring your character strengths to life &
live more fully*. Retrieved from: https://www.viacharacter.org/www/

59   Wrzesniewski, A. & Dutton, J.E. 2001. Crafting a Job: Revisioning
Employees as Active Crafters of Their Work. *Academy of Management
Review*, 26(2), 179-201.

60   Cameron, K. & McNaughtan, J. 2014. Positive Organisational Change.
Journal of Applied Behavioural Science, 50(4), 445-462.

61   Ibid.

62   Kopelman, S., Elana, R., Feldman, D.M. & McDaniel, D.T. 2012. Mindfully
negotiating a career with a heart. *Organizational Dynamics*, 41(2), 163-171.

Chapter 4 Endnotes

63   Crabb, S. 2011. The Use of Coaching Principles to Foster Employee Engagement. *The Coaching Psychologist*, 7(1), 27-34.

64   Kopelman, S., Elana, R., Feldman, D.M. & McDaniel, D.T. 2012. Mindfully negotiating a career with a heart. *Organizational Dynamics*, 41(2), 163-171.

65   Rothmann, S. & Welsh, C. 2013. Employee Engagement: The Role of psychological Conditions. *Management Dynamics*, 22(1), 14-25.

66   Zander, B. & Zander, R.S. 2000. *The Art of Possibility: Transforming Professional and Personal Life*. Boston, MA: Harvard Business School Press, p56.

67   Cartolari, R. 2019. *Traditional Leadership Models Are Losing Relevance: Four Areas To Focus On In 2019*. Retrieved from: https://www.forbes.com/sites/forbescoachescouncil/2019/01/24/traditional-leadership-models-are-losing-relevance-four-areas-to-focus-on-in-2019/#53512ccbef0a

68   Deloitte. 2019. *The Deloitte Global Millennial Survey 2019: Optimism, trust reach troubling low levels*, p13. Retrieved from: https://www2.deloitte.com/global/en/pages/about-deloitte/articles/millennialsurvey.html

69   Ibid.

70   Ibid.

71   Rothmann, S. & Welsh, C. 2013. Employee Engagement: The Role of psychological Conditions. *Management Dynamics*, 22(1), 14-25.

72   Garrad, L. 2017. *How to Make Work More Meaningful for Your Team*. Retrieved from: https://hbr.org/2017/08/how-to-make-work-more-meaningful-for-your-team

73   Sinek, S., Mead, D. & Docker, P. 2017. *Find Your Why: A Practical Guide for Discovering Purpose for You and Your Team*. New York: Penguin Random House.

74   Garrad, L. 2017. *How to Make Work More Meaningful for Your Team*. Retrieved from: https://hbr.org/2017/08/how-to-make-work-more-meaningful-for-your-team

75   Virgin Group. n.d. *Our Purpose*. Retrieved from: https://www.virgin.com/virgingroup/content/our-purpose-0

76   Schawbel, D. 2014. *Richard Branson's Three Most Important Leadership Principles*. Retrieved from: https://www.forbes.com/sites/danschawbel/2014/09/23/richard-branson-his-3-most-important-leadership-principles/#16733f593d50

77   Gallo, C. 2011. *Steve Jobs and the Power of Vision*. Retrieved from: https://www.forbes.com/sites/carminegallo/2011/01/18/steve-jobs-and-the-power-of-vision/#15e33a5b172b

78   Winfrey, O. n.d. *Every Person Has a Purpose*. Retrieved from: https://www.oprah.com/spirit/how-oprah-winfrey-found-her-purpose

79   The Body Shop. 2018. *Our Commitment*. Retrieved from: https://www.thebodyshop.com/en-us/about-us/our-commitment

80   Sortheix, F., Dietrich, J., Chow, A. & Salmela-Aro, K. 2013. The Role of Career Values for Work Engagement during the Transition to Working Life. *Journal of Vocational Behaviour*, 83(3), 466-475.

81   Sinek, S., Mead, D. & Docker, P. 2017. *Find Your Why: A Practical Guide for Discovering Purpose for You and Your Team*. New York: Penguin Random House.

82   Barrett, R. 2010. *The Importance of Values in Building a High-Performance Culture*. Retrieved from: https://www.valuescentre.com/wp-content/uploads/PDF_Resources/Additional_Articles/Article_Importance_of_Values.pdf

83   Ibid.

84   Ibid.

85   Cameron, K. & McNaughtan, J. 2014. Positive Organisational Change. *Journal of Applied Behavioural Science*, 50(4), 445-462.

86   Collins, J.C. 2001. *Good to great: Why some companies make the leap ... and others don't*. New York, NY: HarperBusiness.

87   Crabb, S. 2011. The Use of Coaching Principles to Foster Employee Engagement. *The Coaching Psychologist*, 7(1), 27-34.

88   Posner, B.Z. 2010. Another Look at the Impact of Personal and Organisational Values Congruency. *Journal of Business Ethics*, 97(4), 535-541.

89   Ibid.

90   Patagonia. (n.d.). *We're in business to save our home planet*. Retrieved from: https://www.patagonia.com/company-info.html

91   Bakker, A.B. 2011. An Evidence-Based Model of Work Engagement. *Current Directions in Psychological Science*, 20(4), 265-269.

92   Liu, A. 2019. *Making Joy a Priority at Work*. Retrieved from: https://hbr.org/2019/07/making-joy-a-priority-at-work

Chapter 5 Endnotes

93   Deloitte. 2018. *2018 Deloitte Millennial Survey*. Retrieved from: https://www2.deloitte.com/content/dam/Deloitte/global/Documents/About-Deloitte/gx-2018-millennial-survey-report.pdf

94   Ibid.

95   Mindsetworks. n.d. *Decades of Scientific Research that Started a Growth Mindset Revolution*. Retrieved from: https://www.mindsetworks.com/science/

96   Dweck, C.S. 1988. *Why Do Mindsets Matter?* Retrieved from: https://danerwin.typepad.com/my_weblog/2014/04/dweck.html

97 Buckingham, M. 2005. *What great managers do*. Retrieved from http://hbr.org/2005/03/what-great-managers-do/ar/.

98 Gallup. 2013. *State of the American Workplace Report: Employee Engagement Insights for U.S. Business Leaders*. Washington, D.C.: Gallup, Inc.

99 Ibid.

100 Kolb, D.A. 1983. *Experiential Learning: Experience as the Source of Learning and Development*. Upper Saddle River, New Jersey: Pearson Education.

101 Whitmore, J. 2017. *Coaching for Performance: The Principles and Practice of Coaching and Leadership*. Updated 25th Anniversary Edition. Boston, MA: Nicholas Brealey Publishing.

Chapter 6 Endnotes

102 Harter, J. & Adkins, A. 2015. *Employees Want a Lot More From Their Managers*. Retrieved from: https://www.gallup.com/workplace/236570/employees-lot-managers.aspx

103 Robison, J. 2019. *What Millennials Want is Good for Your Business*. Retrieved from: https://www.gallup.com/workplace/248009/millennials-good-business.aspx?g_source=link_NEWSV9&g_medium=TOPIC&g_campaign=item_&g_content=What%2520Millennials%2520Want%2520Is%2520Good%2520for%2520Your%2520Business

104 Chamorro-Premuzic, T., Wade, M. & Jordan, J. 2018. *As AI Makes More Decisions, the Nature of Leadership Will Change*. Retrieved from: https://hbr.org/2018/01/as-ai-makes-more-decisions-the-nature-of-leadership-will-change

105 Greenleaf, R.K. n.d. *Who is a Servant Leader?* Retrieved from: https://www.greenleaf.org/

106 Mackey, J. & Sisodia, R. 2013. *"Conscious Capitalism" Is Not an Oxymoron*. Retrieved from: https://hbr.org/2013/01/cultivating-a-higher-conscious

107 Barrett, R. 2010. *Leadership Development*. Retrieved from: https://www.valuescentre.com/leadership-development/

108 Goleman, D., Boyatzis, R. & McKee, A. 2002. *Primal Leadership*. Boston, MA: Harvard Business School Press.

109 Giles, S. 2016. *The Most Important Leadership Competencies, According to Leaders around the World*. Retrieved from: https://hbr.org/2016/03/the-most-important-leadership-competencies-according-to-leaders-around-the-world

110 Achor, S. 2013. *Before Happiness*. New York: Crown Business.

111 Fredrickson, B.L. 2004. The Broaden-and-Build Theory of Positive Emotions. *The Royal Society*, 359, 1367-1377.

112 Kaplan, S., Bradley-Geist, J.C., Ahmed, A., Anderson, A., Hargrove, A.K. & Lindsey, A. 2013. A Test of Two Positive Psychology Interventions to Increase Employee Well-Being. *Journal of Business and Psychology*, 29(3), 367-380.

113 Zenger, J. & Folkman, J. 2013. *The Ideal Praise-to-Criticism Ratio*. Retrieved from: https://hbr.org/2013/03/the-ideal-praise-to-criticism

114 HeartMath Institute. n.d. *The Science of HeartMath*. Retrieved from: https://www.heartmath.com/science/

115 Vozza, S. 2014. *Personal Mission Statements Of 5 Famous CEOs (And Why You Should Write One Too)*. Retrieved from: https://www.fastcompany.com/3026791/personal-mission-statements-of-5-famous-ceos-and-why-you-should-write-one-too

Chapter 7 Endnotes

116 Bersin, J. 2015. *Becoming irresistible: A new model for employee engagement*. Retrieved from: https://www2.deloitte.com/insights/us/en/deloitte-review/issue-16/employee-engagement-strategies.html

117 Gallup. 2016. *Gallup Q12 Employee Engagement Survey*. Retrieved from: https://q12.gallup.com/Public/en-us/Features

118 Murphy, M. 2015. *Stop Asking These Questions on Your Employee Engagement Survey*. Retrieved from: https://www.forbes.com/sites/markmurphy/2015/05/04/stop-asking-these-questions-on-your-employee-engagement-survey/#4ab3d6f14fa1

119 Gallup. 2016. *Gallup Q12 Employee Engagement Survey*. Retrieved from: https://q12.gallup.com/Public/en-us/Features

120 Wiles, J. (2018). *9 Questions that Should be in Every Employee Engagement Survey*. Retrieved from: https://www.gartner.com/smarterwithgartner/the-9-questions-that-should-be-in-every-employee-engagement-survey/

121 Dvorak, N. & Pendell, R. 2019. *Want to Change Your Culture? Listen to Your Best People*. Retrieved from: https://www.gallup.com/workplace/247361/change-culture-listen-best-people.aspx?g_source=link_WWWV9&g_medium=TOPIC&g_campaign=item_&g_content=Want%2520to%2520Change%2520Your%2520Culture%3f%2520Listen%2520to%2520Your%2520Best%2520People

Index

V

vision, 27, 36, 81–82, 84–92,
94–103, 106–108, 112–114,
147–153, 161, 163, 170, 172,
176, 209–210, 212–213
vision and values implementation,
97

W

way forward, 4, 78, 136–137, 196
weaknesses, 64, 75
well-being, 2, 6, 15–18, 21–23, 32,
60, 86, 100, 105, 109, 113,
132, 151, 167, 172–173
work and well-being, 17
work climate for engagement, 27
workaholism, 2, 14

www.ingramcontent.com/pod-product-compliance
Lightning Source LLC
Chambersburg PA
CBHW071657200326
41519CB00012BA/2541